The

ART

of

INTUITION

The

ART

of

INTUITION

Cultivating Your Inner Wisdom

SOPHY BURNHAM

JEREMY P. TARCHER/PENGUIN

New York

JEREMY P. TARCHER/PENGUIN
Published by the Penguin Group
Penguin Group (USA) Inc., 375 Hudson Street, New York, New York 10014, USA •
Penguin Group (Canada), 90 Eglinton Avenue East, Suite 700, Toronto, Ontario M4P 2Y3,
Canada (a division of Pearson Penguin Canada Inc.) • Penguin Books Ltd, 80 Strand,
London WC2R 0RL, England • Penguin Ireland, 25 St Stephen's Green, Dublin 2, Ireland
(a division of Penguin Books Ltd) • Penguin Group (Australia), 250 Camberwell Road,
Camberwell, Victoria 3124, Australia (a division of Pearson Australia Group Pty Ltd) •
Penguin Books India Pvt Ltd, 11 Community Centre, Panchsheel Park, New Delhi–110 017,
India • Penguin Group (NZ), 67 Apollo Drive, Rosedale, North Shore 0632, New Zealand
(a division of Pearson New Zealand Ltd) • Penguin Books (South Africa) (Pty) Ltd,
24 Sturdee Avenue, Rosebank, Johannesburg 2196, South Africa

Penguin Books Ltd, Registered Offices: 80 Strand, London WC2R 0RL, England

The author gratefully acknowledges permission to reprint from the following:
The Illuminated Rumi by Jalal Al-Din Rumi, translated by Coleman Barks.
Published by Broadway Books, 1997. Reproduced by permission of the translator.
Quotations from Wolfgang Amadeus Mozart, Neil Simon, and Peter Ilyich Tchaikovsky
from *The Creating Brain: The Neuroscience of Genius* © 2005 Nancy C. Andreasen.
Published by Dana Press, a division of the Dana Foundation. Used by permission.
The Nature of Things by Lucretius, translated by A. E. Stallings (p. 39). Published by
Penguin Books Ltd, 2007. Reproduced by permission of Penguin Books Ltd.

Most Tarcher/Penguin books are available at special quantity discounts for bulk purchase
for sales promotions, premiums, fund-raising, and educational needs. Special books or book
excerpts also can be created to fit specific needs. For details, write Penguin Group (USA)
Inc. Special Markets, 375 Hudson Street, New York, NY 10014.

Library of Congress Cataloging-in-Publication Data

Burnham, Sophy.
The art of intuition : cultivating your inner wisdom / Sophy Burnham.
p.   cm.
ISBN 978-1-58542-849-6
1. Intuition.   2. Psychic ability.   I. Title.
BF315.5.B87   2011   2010036993
133.8—dc22

Printed in the United States of America
1   3   5   7   9   10   8   6   4   2

Book design by Sue Walsh

To George and Mary, for their love,

and to

Adelaide, Beatrice, Georgia, and Rosie,

from the depths of mine

CONTENTS

The
ART
of
INTUITION

PRELUDE

·

It is only with the heart that one can see
rightly. What is essential is invisible to
the eye.

ANTOINE DE SAINT-EXUPÉRY,
The Little Prince

WHEN I WAS A CHILD I'd crouch above the puddles formed by rainwater on our driveway and stare long minutes into those deep pools. The water might have been less than an inch deep, but it exposed a magical world: the sky, the clouds, my own face looking up at me, and high overhead the towering oak trees tearing with their fingers at the clouds. Which was real? Was it I, staring into the depths of the rain-puddle world? Or was the girl who looked out from the water the real one, watching an imaginary me?

After my books *A Book of Angels* and *Angel Letters* were published, people around the world wrote me, and invariably they asked about spirits and ghosts, and offered their own curious tales of intuition. How do you increase your intuition, learn to hear your spirit guides? Do we become angels when we die? Are there evil, scary spirits? And always, at the root of the questions, is the Great Doubt: What happens to us when we die? When does "life" begin?

When I was a young woman, my grandmother, then in her

eighties, turned to me. I still remember where she stood on the rag rug in her farmhouse, the look in her haunted eyes.

"I'm so afraid of dying," she said. I fled. For years it lay on my conscience that I had let her down. Today, years later, I'd know what to say. "Of course you're afraid," I'd answer. "You'd be nuts if you weren't." Or perhaps I'd say something else. The story line changes according to my mood.

"It's all right," I'd say. "There is no death; you are eternal. Even your personality survives. All you'll do is shed the physical body, skin and bones, but the essence of *you* lives on."

Or perhaps, if I had it to do over, I would just listen to her. I would ask about her fears. I would hold her doubt in sacred space. There is healing in deep listening, too.

I have written much about the spiritual dimension. *The Ecstatic Journey* is about mystical experiences and about the ringing joy that changes you thereafter; *The Path of Prayer* is about the energy of Thought and how Intention draws our fate mysteriously toward us, that is, what you think is what you get. I have written novels that consider the mystifying questions of good and evil, and how to find hope in the midst of horror, violence, and the unimaginable cruelties we inflict on one another—the monstrous suffering of ordinary life.

This book takes up intuition and the higher sense perceptions, which all mystics agree are the natural by-products of the Spiritual Awakening. And if the subject moves from hunches to seeing auras or sensing an invisible presence, from mysticism to sudden inexplicable insights, it's because all these topics are part of one continuum, like the slide of a trombone, guiding us to the Divine. This book, then—let us be clear—is about connecting with the wild, majestic, ineffable, and numinous force that we call God, Allah, the Buddha, the Tao, Shiva, Christ, the Universe, Providence, and by a thousand other names.

It is my contention that psychic abilities are as natural as the blink of our eyes, and they can be developed with practice. Like the mystical experience itself, they bring a pure and heart-ringing happiness, a confidence in living, a sense of joy—of crying *Yes, Yes!* to life. The spiritual awakening brings a falling away of anxiety and fear, a heightened awareness of beauty and goodness, coupled always with gratitude, humility, and a sweet, unselfish interest in others.

This book, therefore, is about alerting you to *powers you already have*. It is also about grace falling drop by drop into our daily lives.

As soon as you trust yourself, you will know how to live.

JOHANN WOLFGANG VON GOETHE

HOW MANY PEOPLE have had a spiritual experience? More than we will ever know; for most people never reveal what they have seen. They live quietly, and you don't even know their hearts are bursting with celestial fire. Barbara Bradley Hagerty, in her beautiful work *Fingerprints of God*, writes that 51 percent of Americans claim to have had a mystical or ecstatic experience of God. But 90 percent of Americans believe in God, and I suspect that figure to be higher.

Have one, and the event is seared into your mind: You will never forget the date and time of the event, and afterward . . . you are different. Your brain is different. You may have healing touch, shamanic powers. You may become highly psychic, intuitive, and certainly your entire attitude toward life will have changed.

Moses went up to the mountaintop and returned so shining with light that we're told he had to cover his face with a veil. This is hyped-up storytelling, of course, good metaphor, but light is part of the experience: You shine with light, rivers of light running off your hands. Moreover, you see light flaring off the grasses, trees, hills, animals—everything glowing with light, and so, too, are all the people around you. There are many kinds of spiritual experiences. Some are so delicate, so fragile, that you hardly know anything happened, until you look back five years later and realize how different you are, how much you've changed since then. Other mystical encounters are so majestic that they rend your life asunder. You cannot return to your old ways—or even to the people you once knew. You have been visited by angels or carried, like Saint Paul, to the third of the seven heavens of Sumerian myth. You've been touched by the Divine. You've found your Self. With a capital S.

The mystical encounter brings confusion, discomfort, difficulty, but it also brings hope, forgiveness, limitless compassion, humility, gratitude, and a sense of one-ness with everything around you. It brings an unselfish interest in others. You are free. Years ago I wrote a poem about it:

> *I have seen the earth*
> *Shining,*
> *Flashing with light divine.*
> *But more wondrous is this:*
> *To observe*
> *With awe*
> *Just common grime.*

And one of its side effects is the acquisition of sharp intuition, heightened or psychic perceptions. We call them paranormal. The prefix *para-* comes from the Greek, meaning "beside," "alongside," "near," and also "beyond," as in "beyond the normal." It has much

the same connotation as *meta*, as in *metaphysical*. But the paranormal may in fact be utterly normal, mundane.

LISTEN. LISTEN. That is what we are asked to do. And when
we listen quietly, we find how much we are loved by the Beloved—
angels, spirits, guides, guardians, totems—by whatever name we
call these messengers of the Divine. I make no bones about it: I
believe in a spirit world. I have seen with my own eyes that the
soul lives on after the passage that we call death. To anyone who
still questions, however, anyone still riven by skepticism and
doubt, I hope this book brings insight and delight; to those who
grieve the loss of a loved one, peace; and to those who are afraid
of dying, hope.

Scientists tell us that we humans use only a tiny fraction of
our brains, the rest of the cells just rocking on the back porch
apparently, feet up on a crate, smoking and spitting, waiting for
the clatter of the fire alarm to bring along some fun. What I'm
suggesting is that those sleeping cerebral cells hold the gifts of
prophecy and intuition—of healing touch, telepathy, and remote
viewing, of animal communication, psychokinesis, teleportation,
of seeing into the spiritual dimensions, communing with your
inner wisdom—the mystery of God.

I think of accessing these abilities like tuning in to a radio
frequency. As you raise your vibration by prayer and purity of
heart, you become more sensitive and you "hear" without the
static of your surroundings or the chatter of your own racketing
monkey-mind. These heightened sensitivities are gifts to be held
in deep humility, knowing they should never be used for personal
power but only for serving others. The Hindus call them *siddhis*.

Great teachers say that they are dangerous and should not
be taught to the uninitiated. "Don't dabble," a wise man once

warned me. I agree, for who doesn't know the story of Dr. Faustus, who sold his soul to the Devil in return for knowledge? Great souls say that these spiritual secrets should be transmitted only one on one, from master to student, mouth to ear, or else absorbed by osmosis, as it were, merely by sitting in the presence of an enlightened being, resonating to that vibration. For the *siddhi*s are glamorous, seductive, and their siren song can entice you from the Way and into tangled underbrush.

But we enter a new era.

I have confidence in the goodness, courage, wisdom, and nobility of people. I think we are evolving as a species, and the time has come to speak of secret things, to spread them like jewels at our feet, and string them round our necks and arms, hang them from our ears, and wind them in our hair like royal diadems. God is only a heartbeat away, and so too these designations of divinity.

Part I

THE STILL, SMALL VOICE OF GOD

Is it arrogant, presumptuous, to think that I might have heard the Voice of God? Not at all. We all do—that "still, small voice" that we speak of, telling us what we ought to do. That, I think, is the Voice of God. Of course, it is usually called the voice of conscience, and if we feel more comfortable with that definition, that's fine.

JANE GOODALL, *Reason for Hope*

one

MYSTERIOUS KNOWINGS

We all have a better guide in ourselves,
if we would attend to it, than any other
person can be.

JANE AUSTEN

YEARS AGO, when I was a young woman working as a contributing editor at *Town & Country,* the magazine sent me on assignment to Costa Rica. The first night there, I attended a barbecue hosted by the organization I was writing about, and I remember standing under the tall, dark trees with a sweet, balmy wind ruffling my hair, just looking about, content to watch the crowd. The yellow glow of torches and the red fire from the huge hot barbecue cast black shadows across the scene, so that people seemed to rise from the night and fall back like specters. The night air was soft and dark as dreams.

Behind me, at my ear, I heard a startled male voice: "Oh, you're going to be famous." I turned to see a white-bearded older man.

I burst out laughing. "That's the best pickup line I've ever heard." For being famous is no sane ambition: Charles Manson, the mass murderer, was famous, after all, Jack the Ripper, Osama bin Laden.

"No, no. It's true," he said, and now I could hear the Scottish accent. "My grandmother was a seer, and I've inherited the gift from her. Every Sunday there'd be a line out the door of people waiting for the free readings that she gave after church on Sundays. I thought everyone's grandmother gave readings, was a seer."

His name was Ian McPhail, and he introduced me to two friends of his, Bill Jordan, an Irish vet who later created a wildlife organization, Care for the Wild, and Felipe Benavides, a Peruvian aristocrat who was deeply involved with the preservation of the Paracus Peninsula and the vicuña in the high Andes. We spent the next three days together.

I was enthralled. Never before had I heard grown men talk openly of God or loving kindness, or express their concern for plants and animals and the habitats in which they lived. Today, thirty years later, these are common themes, defending wildlife, saving the environment, but at the time this was way-out stuff. I'd never heard a macho American accept as natural and normal the underbelly of scientific lore—those inexplicable moments of intuition, insight, and telepathy that accompany the mystical journey into the Divine. We told stories late into the night.

Ian told me about an Australian friend of his who owned a sheep station so large that he'd named the outlying areas London, Edinburgh, and Plymouth. An aborigine brilliant with animals worked for him. Whatever the aborigine asked, the horse or ewe or dog would do. He seemed to know their very thoughts. The man was invaluable. The only thing is, he refused to work the whole year. One day, he would come to the boss and say, "It's time to go."

The rancher knew better than to argue. The next morning they would get in the jeep and drive for hours into the trackless bush, his workman pointing the way. Then, in the middle of nowhere, he'd say, "Stop." He'd get out of the car, take off his shirt, pants, shoes, socks, underwear—fold them neatly, and place them on the seat of the jeep.

"Okay." He'd stand buck naked. "Meet you here. In seven months."

Then he would sniff the wind and trot off into the barren outback to join his nomad family. He would wander with them for half a year, but on the appointed day, there he'd be, waiting for the boss to pick him up. He'd put on his clothes and go back to work.

How did he know where his family was as it roamed across that wilderness?

How did he know when to go back to work, or even where to meet his boss?

Ian had been an airman as a youth in World War II. He told me he could look at the young men flying out on a mission that night and know which would come back and which would be shot down and killed. He'd see a darkness surrounding the laughing, chosen man, as if the shadow of death hovered behind.

"What did you do?"

"Nothing. Of course, I never said anything. But I was always right."

It was in this period that he began to write. "It was like a finger poking me in the back," he told me. "Poems came pouring out, one after another. And then one day they stopped. I haven't written another since."

They had a profound effect on me, these three men. They opened me to an inner world that I'd tried hard to ignore, and when I went home to my husband and children, I felt confused and torn by conflicting loyalties. All my life I'd struggled to use principally the gifts of Reason, which, since the Enlightenment of the eighteenth century, have marked our culture as "civilized." All my life I'd tried to tamp down the irrational, dark, dangerous, uncontrollable eruptions of intuition.

Fifty-one percent of Americans claim to have had a mystical experience; 90 percent believe in God.

WE HEAR MANY STORIES of so-called primitive people. Laurens van der Post lived with the Kalahari Bushmen in Botswana and described how the men would leave the village on a hunt. They might be gone for days, but suddenly one day back home there would be joyous activity and preparation of the fires.

"The men have killed a gazelle. They're bringing meat."

To the anthropologist this telepathy was mystifying. To the San, an indigenous people, a telegraph, with its poles and wires, is probably a matter for ridicule when extrasensory perception (ESP) works just fine.

Intuition. Insight. Precognition. Clairvoyance. Today I've come to accept these qualities the way I accept that the sun, that rolling, roiling ball of fire, will come up tomorrow: not because I understand the motions of the earth and sun as we spin through vast cosmic systems, moving a million miles a day along the edges of the Milky Way (100 billion stars that form a galaxy 100,000 light-years wide), but because of its simple dailyness. It feels so ordinary that I use the word "understand," when what I mean is, "am familiar with." The same is true of instantaneous, unreflective apprehension.

What is intuition? A hunch, a gut feeling, an inspiration, or a premonition, precognition, clairvoyance, clairaudience, clairsentience, prescience, second sight—the shiver of "knowing" that pierces the veil of time and peers briefly into the future or at least into what's not happened yet. It's a decision made so fast you don't know how you reached it: "It came to me," you say. The root of *intuition* is related to the word *tuition*, from the Latin *tueri*, meaning "to guard, to protect." For no rational reason we suddenly know: "Go here, not there!" Or sometimes: "*Stop!*" If we're alert, we respond instantly, because intuition is always right.

The CEO who suddenly sells a stock "on a hunch" never pauses perhaps to wonder how he knew. He boasts of his smarts, attributing the sale to experience, intellect. On the other hand, the woman who shies in revulsion from a man in the doorway isn't aware that she is reading a host of microsignals, including the energy field that surrounds him, his aura, or that in that first flash of intuition she "knows" him. Later, when he approaches her, all charm and smiles, asking her to dance, when he arouses her pity with his sad life story and sweeps her off her feet with flowers and chocolates . . . her rational mind has already clouded her original knowledge. And only as she ends the abusive and violent marriage does she remember that she knew everything about him on first sight, that reason overrode her instinct.

WHERE DOES THE INFORMATION come from? Is there an intuition place in the brain, like the orgasmic G-spot? Are women more intuitive than men? Are men and women intuitive about different matters or in different realms? Can intuition be developed?

Sometimes a definition is easier to mark by what it is not. Joanne, a brilliant journalist, offered her own experience to prove that intuition can't be trusted. One day while waiting at the doctor's office, she saw that the only other waiting patient was an unkempt, disreputable-looking woman, the more off-putting for having the shadow of a dark moustache. Joanne shuddered at the idea of talking to her! But as time passed and the boredom increased, they gradually fell into conversation, where to Joanne's surprise the woman turned out to be a nuclear physicist, and captivating.

"There's an example of how you can't trust your intuition," she finished. "I thought she was the last person on earth I'd want to talk to, and instead she was fascinating."

But that wasn't intuition. Joanne had made her judgment based on intellect, not intuition. Intuition creeps in shyly to the noisy barn dance on ballet slippers so soft that you hardly hear them whisper against the floor. We recognize it most often in times of crisis and danger, those moments, rare and dramatic, when it saves your life or offers prescience you cannot understand. By definition intuition involves information unavailable to the intellect, and it is always to be trusted.

The one problem with intuition is that while it gives you a nudge or hesitation or signals to go here or there, it cannot tell you WHY! Intuition warns you that something in the future is "wrong" for you, but it cannot tell you what! Perhaps you've been invited on a wonderful adventure with friends. You want to go, yet you hesitate, drag your heels, can't bring yourself to commit! Your conscious mind wants to join them; your intuition whispers no.

How hard it is to hear!

Or act on it.

Often intuition makes no *sense*!

I have a friend whose mother was engaged to a young man who loved cinder-path motorcycle racing, a dangerous sport. She signed up to go on a cruise with her family, while her fiancé entered his last big race. Then intuition intervened. Anxiety. She canceled the cruise and insisted that her fiancé forgo his cinder-path race. He loaned his motorcycle to a friend to take his place. The cruise ship sank. The friend was killed in the race.

But my friend's mother knew nothing of that future event . . . only the tingling sense of urgency, a quiver that something wasn't right.

Perhaps you'll never know what was "not right." Your friends will go on their adventure and come back healthy, having had a stupendous time! You missed out. And yet you have to trust your intuition. Always.

SOME LUCKY PEOPLE ARE aware of their hunches; they are born with "the gift," not knowing that these abilities are skills that can be learned and practiced, just as you learn to think or play the piano or do crossword puzzles.

My computer specialist, Mike, comes from a family of intuitives. Once, when he was a young man, he came home from school, slamming the screen door behind him.

"How was Susan?" his mother called to him.

"How did you know about Susan?"

"I guess you mentioned her," she answered guiltily.

"We need to talk," he challenged her.

"What about?"

"I only met her an hour ago."

"Oh." His mother turned. "Okay. We need to talk. I have this gift. You have it. Your sister has it. Never, never let anyone know! Never talk about it. It's a curse, not a gift!"

The root of *intuition* is in the Latin *tueri*, which means "to guard, to protect."

SO IMPERIOUS IS INTUITION, and so mysterious, that the U.S. Army is now studying the phenomenon. "Something's wrong," the soldier thinks, and pulls up short, for an intuition is more to be trusted than even a robotic bomb sniffer. A hunch can save your life. What is it? How does it work?

Carl Jung spoke of the collective unconscious. Rupert Sheldrake suggests we operate in "morphic fields," and Max Planck, the physicist, spoke of the matrix behind all matter. In his entertaining book *Blink*, the Canadian journalist Malcolm Gladwell proposes that intuition is the result of the "adaptive unconscious," which is that part of the brain that leaps to instant and brilliant conclusions. (Don't you love the way scientists make up new terms for perfectly adequate ones?) Gladwell is interested in those decisions made in the blink of an eye. He tells how the Getty Museum in Los Angeles was about to spend $10 million for a magnificent *kouros*, a beautiful Greek statue of a standing boy, fists clasped at his thighs. A battery of scientific tests had already validated its absolute authenticity, but when Thomas Hoving, former director of the Metropolitan Museum in New York, saw it, the first words that popped into his mind were *fresh* and *wrong*. Federico Zeri and Evelyn Harrison, two authorities, agreed. Georgios Dontas, head of the Archaeological Society in Athens, went cold when he saw the work. "I felt as though there was a glass between me and the work." Another felt a shudder of intuitive repulsion. These authorities could not really explain how they knew it was a fake. They simply had an "educated eye."

Gladwell calls such snap decisions the "thin slicing" of information by the brain, and he describes test after test, illustrating the swiftness of such pattern recognition. Observers following a married couple's conversation on any neutral subject for one hour can predict with 95 percent accuracy whether the marriage will last for fifteen years. Only *fifteen minutes* of observation yields a reading that's 90 percent accurate. Students watching a videotape of a teacher speaking nothing but garbled nonsense syllables can predict within *two seconds* with 90 percent accuracy whether the teacher is good or not.

The rest of Gladwell's book suggests that instantaneous decidement is simply the educated brain whipping through reams of information like a giant computer and coming up with judgments so fast they seem to have been made in a flash. It's a survival skill. In times of danger, he says, you don't want to have to stop and reflect: You *jump!* He points out that first impressions are not always right (this is not my experience, by the way), that unconscious bias comes into play, especially concerning the opposite sex or color or race or cultural distinctions. We override our instincts by what psychologist Jonathan Schooler calls verbal overshadowing.

One of Gladwell's most interesting observations concerns damage to the ventromedial prefrontal area of the brain, behind the nose. This is the decision-making center, and damage to this area causes "a disconnect between what you know and what you do." You can't make a decision; you have neither intuition nor reflection, or else you pore over the material endlessly, knowing *what* to do but never arriving at the impulse to act.

The ancient Hindus spoke of the Akashic River of Knowledge that sages dip into now and again. I remember reading years ago of Rupert Sheldrake's "morphic fields," an invisible medium in which all information floats. Sheldrake tells one story of how, after years of effort by scientists to create in the laboratory a totally new crystal, they finally succeeded . . . after which the "artificial" crystal could easily be duplicated anywhere in the world, as if the first one served as a spiritual template for all others; and he recounted how, after one group of lab rats in London mastered a difficult maze, their offspring, the next generation, knew it automatically. But how? (I might add that Sheldrake created a storm of controversy, and charges in *Nature* that his thesis is pseudoscience.)

Also around this time the hundred-monkey syndrome started to make the rounds. The story began with an isolated island off the coast of Japan that served as a research station for monkeys. Because the island didn't produce enough food, extra supplies were periodically dropped down to the monkeys by plane. One day, one genius young female monkey took a dropped yam down to the ocean and washed the sand off in the sea before eating it. Not only was her yam clean, but it also had a pleasant salty taste. No other monkeys washed their food, but this one female always did, and she taught her young to wash their food as well. Soon their playmates began to imitate the action, so that a whole generation of young monkeys washed its food.

At some point the yam-washing number reached a critical mass (call it ninety-nine monkeys washing their yams), while the rest of the population still held out. And then the hundredth monkey carried a yam down to the sea and washed it in the salty waves. The scale tipped. Suddenly every monkey on the island, young and old, began to wash its food. Today we call it the tipping point.

Is this what will happen with us, as more and more people become aware of our intuition, of prescient dreams and creative premonitions? For intuition can come in many forms. When the "knowing" relates to the present we call it intuition. When the insight concerns the future, we call it precognition, prescience, or presentiment. When it concerns thought transference, we name it mental telepathy. But aren't they all aspects of the same ability, and does it matter if the information comes in a dream or during meditation, while showering or working quietly in the garden?

Elizabeth Whiteley is a Washington, D.C., painter and sculptor. She told me that artists sometimes paint the future, as she herself has done. On one occasion, after moving to a new apartment, she recognized the view from one of the windows as being the very image she had painted ten years earlier. On another occasion, she was nearly killed in a sailing accident when a motorboat rammed her vessel. Thrown into the water, near drowning, she was struck by the special green color of the water. Later, thinking she should paint away her trauma, she discovered she had already painted the scene, employing exactly that unusual green, a tone she had never used before.

In 1999, Michael Richards, an African-American sculptor, completed a bronze statue of a black Saint Sebastian pierced by flying airplanes. Two years later, while working in his studio on the ninety-second floor of South Tower of the World Trade Center, he was one of the thousands killed by terrorists in hijacked airplanes, and much of his work was destroyed. As for writers, we don't have to look far to find prescient imagination. Back to the World Trade Center, it was in a Tom Clancy novel that planes first flew into the towers.

LARRY DOSSEY, in his book *The Power of Premonitions*, gives another explanation of intuition and precognition: The mind, he says, is "nonlocal," and though lodged in the brain and locked inside the skull, it has the ability to sweep out beyond time and space to grasp at everything and everywhere. The term *nonlocal* comes from physics. According to the old world order, Time always and consistently moves forward, but Dossey notes that in theory Time can move in any direction—backward, forward, sideways—exposing all information to the infinite, unhindered power of the "nonlocal" mind.

Dossey's book is filled with stories of ordinary people foreseeing catastrophic events, and this is so common both in folklore and in scientific studies that you'd think it would hardly rouse comment. The events of 9/11, for example, generated the largest outpouring of disaster premonitions ever received at the Rhine Research Center in Durham, North Carolina, which has collected more than fourteen thousand cases of intuition and extrasensory perception since the 1920s. (The spike was followed, curiously, by a big drop-off in premonitions only hours before the event itself. Why? Is that because at a certain moment there's no longer time to take advantage of the portent, change plans? Or because the *event* has become fixed somehow, memorable?)

Even more startling, however, is the fact that, apparently, based on their inexplicable cognitions, people changed their behavior. Dossey reports that 79 percent of the planes used as weapons of attack that fateful September day had not been full: a chance of one in a million. American Airlines Flight 11, the Boeing 767 that crashed into the North Tower, had room for 168 passengers, but only 92 people were aboard that day; United Flight 175, which hurtled into the South Tower, could likewise have carried 168 passengers but had only 65 people aboard—a 67 percent passenger vacancy rate; while the Boeing 757 that crashed in Pennsylvania was around 80 percent unoccupied, with only 37 of 182 passenger seats filled. When was the last time you or anyone you know flew in a plane with two-thirds of the seats unfilled? One of the people who changed her flight that day was Jean Houston, the renowned psychic.

One study from the 1950s found that trains involved in accidents carried fewer riders on the days of accidents than on other days. In 1912 when the *Titanic* made her maiden (and final) crossing of the Atlantic, many people had forebodings. It sailed unfilled. J. P. Morgan was one of those who canceled his *Titanic* passage on a hunch.

At this point I have to report that I was one of many people who changed a flight that was scheduled for the day of September 11, 2001. I was supposed to fly from New Mexico back to Washington, D.C., but a few weeks beforehand I began to experience such anxiety, such tooth-chattering, gut-churning, sickening nausea at the thought of flying on that day, that I finally paid a $100 fee to change my ticket and come home one day early, on September 10. The moment I rebooked the reservation, all fretting vanished. I was mystified. I had an uneventful flight, arriving home only to wake the next morning and watch in anguish with the rest of the world as the Twin Towers collapsed repeatedly on TV. Later I walked down the hill from my house to the Potomac River, where a pillar of smoke rose above the trees from the Pentagon. I had had a premonition—and acted on it—but I did not foresee the burning towers, the crash of planes, and I'm left wondering *why*? Why is one ordinary woman saved from the minor inconvenience of airport closings, an inability to get home? And what of the 2,973 people who died in the attacks? I've asked several psychics about 9/11, and none foresaw the tragedy. Dossey, however, reports at least two premonitions of destruction and smoke, though they came to no one who could avert the attacks.

"Is there a difference," my sister asked, "between premonition and intuition?" When she was first married, she and her husband went to lunch at his parents' apartment. Driving home, her husband murmured, "I have a feeling I'm never going to see my father again." A week later his father died.

My friend Jane Vessel, when asked about intuition, stared

into the distance thoughtfully. "Yes. It's usually a rare and dramatic moment that I notice," she mused. "The kind that sends me into prayer."

INTUITION IS DIFFERENT FROM FEAR. Intuition comes to each of us in its own personal way. Perhaps it's a nagging sense that something's wrong, though you can't put your finger on it: as when in a dream you've lost something and you're searching for you-don't-know-what. Sometimes it's an odd lassitude or lethargy, a paralyzing inability to act, the hesitation being itself the warning that you're about to take a false step. Sometimes it comes as a physical sensation, a gut-wrenching kick to the belly, the hair rising on your arms, goose bumps, a shudder, or the tingling of your scalp.

As a child I learned to play chess. After some years I quit. I found that during a game my heart would start beating so hard I couldn't think. My hands would shake, and sometimes spots would appear before my eyes. Also, I always lost.

In recent years I've started playing again and I've found all the same symptoms, but far from being a hindrance I've recognize these physical manifestations as signals of intuition: I'm about to make a wrong move. Moreover, now that I'm listening, *aware*, the symptoms don't manifest with such virulence. If my heart beats *thump!* I pause. I breathe. I reexamine the board. My Higher Self knows what my mind can't yet see: I'm about to make a bad move; there's another solution to the trap.

You have to listen for the tuning fork of insight. Honor it. It comes from your Highest Self, the Source. *Even when it makes no sense . . . you must act on it.*

Once I agreed to voluntary surgery. This was in the early eighties, before the AIDS epidemic, before most people (including myself) had even heard the term. The doctor was ready to schedule the operation in two weeks, but I put him off. "No, if I'm going to do this, I need two pints of my own blood for a transfusion."

Where did those words come from? I heard them spill from my lips with a shiver of surprise.

The doctor smiled with patient tolerance. "You won't need a transfusion. I can guarantee that. This is a very simple operation. I've done hundreds."

Nonetheless, I had a bee in my bonnet. I went to the Red Cross and insisted on having a pint of blood drawn and put aside in my name. Six or eight weeks later they gathered the second pint. At the hospital, the night before surgery, I asked if the two pints of blood had been delivered. The nurse said no, but not to worry; I wouldn't need it.

"Well, send a courier for it," I commanded. "Because I'm not having surgery without it."

"But you're scheduled for seven a.m. tomorrow!" she protested.

"Tough. If my own blood is not on hand, I'm walking out of here. I refuse the surgery."

They sent for the blood. To the doctor's surprise, he had to use both pints.

Later, one of the nurses asked me about it: "How did you know to do that?" she inquired. "What a good idea. I think everyone should do that before surgery." A year later, and we were in a full-blown AIDS epidemic with everyone aware of the transmission of the disease through ordinary blood transfusion.

Sometimes an intuition is almost too fragile to hear. A Finnish friend told me of her boyfriend, who, while dressing for work one morning, kept thinking in a niggling way about water . . .

cars. What was it? Water . . . cars? On the way to work, his car stalled. It had run out of water.

Ah, but some are more than niggling knowings.

Jane Rottier, now eighty-three years old, says she used to have premonitory dreams and doesn't anymore. She remembers one time when she was around twenty-five years old. She'd been writing letters. She lay down to nap and dreamed that her brother, who was in the military, would be home for Christmas. In her dream she saw him carrying three suitcases. He set them down on the front steps, calling, "Mama, Mama!"

When she woke up, she told her mother, "I think Bob's coming home for Christmas." That night at two in the morning, she was awoken by a rattling sound. Looking out the window, she saw her brother standing in the snow with three suitcases at his feet. He was throwing pebbles at her window. It annoyed him that his sister had spoiled his Christmas surprise.

"But I don't have premonitions anymore," she reported. "Is that my age?"

As a child, the writer Perry Stieglitz always knew when his father, a traveling man, was coming home.

"Daddy's coming."

"Don't be silly, boy," his mother would say. But moments later his father would be at the door. Animals have this gift as well, and we see it in our own pets: the dog who suddenly leaps up and starts pacing at the doorway while his master is getting off the bus three blocks away; the cat who curls discreetly in the front hall, too dignified to make the fuss of a dog—their intuitions carried on the seeds of love.

Children are highly attuned. I remember my mother taking my sister and me to the trotting races one summer evening. I don't know how old I was, ten, perhaps? Eleven? We shared one program that gave the names of the horses, owners, jockeys, and colors. I remember that I chose the winner for every race except one, when my sister demanded the horse I'd chosen: "I was going to pick that one!" And my mother's cajoling voice: "Let her have it; you've won every time." Her horse won, and my second choice came in second. We didn't bet, of course, but the party behind us leaned forward, you can be sure, to hear which horse the child picked, and I think they may have won some serious money that night.

I said earlier that you must always trust your intuition. This is true, unless you interrupt the perfect machinery of your mind. If you are taking drugs, if you are addicted to alcohol, if you are in emotional distress, angry, vengeful, or overwhelmed by grief— be cautious. Test your intuitions, for all of these (and especially the mind-altering substances) can intervene, and then you are baffled by things that you once knew intuitively how to handle.

IN BLINK, Malcolm Gladwell explains these inexplicable moments of sheer knowing (you can almost hear his sigh of relief) as no more than the swift workings of the "educated eye." But his explanation falls far short. I mentioned the Irish vet Bill Jordan, who became famous for his work in saving wildlife and increasing public awareness of the cruelty inflicted in countless ways on mute and helpless animals. When he was a young medical student in Edinburgh, he went to his oral exams and to his surprise he couldn't make a mistake. He knew it all! As if the responses were whispered by angels into his ear. He knew the questions the examiners were about to ask, as well as the best responses. He was in the flow. In the zone. Inspired. Perhaps you've had such moments while playing tennis or golf, or as an artist when, captured by the Muse, you feel yourself lifted to the heights of creative exaltation. Is that, too, a sample of "thin-slicing" by the "adaptive unconscious," the work of the "educated eye"?

There is a word for these other psychic experiences: *psi*. The term, coined in 1942 by British psychologist Robert Thouless, describes abilities that have baffled scientists since the early 1800s. *Psi* (pronounced "sigh") is related to the Greek word *psyche*, meaning "soul or spirit," and it defines the four ways of receiving information or perceptions without the normal five senses plus two ways in which your thoughts influence events. These six qualities may be related to intuition, or perhaps they are different aspects of the single gift, but surely they belong in our discussion of the phenomenon.

There are two kinds of *psi*:

Perceptions include clairvoyance, clairaudience, clairsentience, telepathy, precognition, premonition, psychic readings, psychometry.

Projections involving mind over matter include psychic surgery, healing touch, levitation, materialization or dematerialization, and other matters not included in this book.

There are four ways of receiving: (1) With *telepathy*, or thought transference, information moves mentally from person to person across space; (2) with *clairvoyance*, you view or "see" a distant event; (3) with *clairaudience* you hear the information, sometimes even as an external voice murmuring in your ear; (4) with *clairsentience* you experience a physical sensation, that is, you feel what is going on in the body of your friend, or you reach a medical diagnosis by sensing the pain of another in your own body.

In addition to these four subtle ways of receiving information, another quality falls under the umbrella of *psi*. With your own focused intention, known as psychokinesis (PK), you are not receiving but projecting. You are able to: bend spoons, move cigarettes around a tabletop, walk on fire without being burned, sleep like an Indian fakir on a bed of nails, or pierce your cheeks with thorns, your belly with swords without bleeding or wounds or scars; or you "send" healing energy and prayer to a person who is ill or in pain. We think of Christ healing the lepers and the blind man or even the centurion's daughter from afar, and we remember His injunction that "this and more shall you do in my name." We all have this ability, if we have the capacity to love. In labs at the Princeton School of Engineering, literally millions of experiments have demonstrated that *by thought alone* anyone can influence highly calibrated, random-operating *machines*— nonsentient matter. Distance makes no difference. You can send an intention from Australia to one of the random-operating machines in Princeton, New Jersey, and at statistically significant levels you have influenced the results. Time makes no difference. You can send your intention ten days before the machine makes a "run," and your intention will be recognized. More astonishing, you can send your intention *after* the machine has produced its results, and if the data have not yet been reviewed and recorded, your intention will be evidenced at statistically significant levels!

These two abilities, then—heightened perception and powerful thought projections—form the basis of *psi*.

It should be noted that everyone has both *perceptive* and *projective* abilities. Mental telepathy, for example, requires two people using the two different skills: a sender and a receiver. The *sender* is using the projective ability, the *receiver* the perceptive one. The two skills are always discrete: You can send or receive, but never at the same time.

In this book I use the terms *intuition* and *premonition* interchangeably. They may be different, but only in degree. In the same way many concepts that we call *psychic* are no more than gradations of ordinary intuition.

two

RIBBONS OF LOVE

All day I think about it, then at night I
say it. Where did I come from, and what
am I supposed to be doing? My soul is
from elsewhere, I'm sure of that . . . Who
says words with my mouth? Who looks
out with my eyes? What is the soul? . . .
If I could taste one sip of an answer, I
could break out of this prison for
drunks. . . . Whoever brought me here
will have to take me home.

JALAL AD-DIN RUMI

ASK ANYONE, even a stranger on the bus, and you'll get a tale of
inexplicable illumination, the bolt from the blue, or intuition. I
was talking to Elise, one of my fellow physical therapy patients
(broken arm: horse), who told me that when she was in college
at Randolph-Macon, her roommate's troubled boyfriend had
once telephoned at two o'clock in the morning, looking for his
girl. Her roommate was out, but hearing the desperation in the
young man's voice, Elise told him to wait, not to hang up, that
she'd go find his girlfriend. There were several obvious places to
look: the library, the art building, where students worked late at
night, the student center. Instead she found herself moving
to the room of a mutual friend. "Do you know where Mary is?"

she asked, and stumbled upon her next door. What intuition led her there?

Often a premonition comes in dreams. One woman told me she had a vivid dream of losing her wallet in London. Yet even in the dream she knew she wasn't in London, for if she had been, she'd have carried her wallet in her waistband as she always did when traveling in a foreign country. On waking, she didn't understand the dream at all. Until later that week, when her friend Judy telephoned to report that she had lost her wallet in London and how upset she was; and then my friend realized that so connected was she to Judy that in her sleep, with her conscious mind turned off, she'd picked up images of her friend's distress.

HOW DO WE KNOW THESE THINGS? What's going on? In his engaging book *Entangled Minds: Extrasensory Experiences in a Quantum Reality,* Dean Radin, senior scientist at the Institute of Noetic Sciences (IONS) in Petaluma, California, suggests it's evidence of *subatomic entanglement,* a term coined in 1935 by Nobel laureate physicist Erwin Schrödinger to describe a particular connection between quantum systems—and now we can't continue without the briefest (and crudest) explanation of what it means to affirm that "the wave functions of particles are entangled." Quantum mechanics describes physical behavior from atomic to cosmological domains as a vast web of particles (or waves) all interlacing from the first moments of Big Bang creation to the present nanosecond, and all remaining in contact across the boundaries of Time and Space. Entangled photons are in a kind of grey area. Einstein, who was skeptical about quantum mechanics, derided it as allowing "spooky action at a distance," which he believed could not be possible. But physicists put it to the test, for example, by sending two particles that had been created in the same event to two locations many miles apart and observing whether each would do its own merry thing or if each somehow "knew" what the other was doing. Turns out they knew. It is not as simple as one photon turning right when the other does, but unimpeachable evidence demonstrates the connection. (So Einstein was right in saying it was spooky but wrong in concluding it couldn't be true or that quantum mechanics must be wrong as well.)

What do the particles "do?" If two particles are created in the same event, their combined spin is often known, while the spin of either one is unknown. If you measure the spin of one particle and find it is plus one, then you immediately know that the other must have a spin of minus one (because the sum of the spins is zero). That remains true as long as the two continue to be "entangled" (meaning they don't collide with other things, or deviate, attracted by the wink and wiggle of a closer, more seductive photon, as they would if they were in air instead of a vacuum). And this holds true for miles. In May 2009, physicists transmitted a pair of entangled photons from La Palma to Tenerife, a distance of about ninety miles. It was an important milestone in the effort to transmit entangled photons from a satellite.

What does all this mean? First, it suggests that the connection occurs through "other" dimensions. Indeed, modern (super) string theory says that there may be ten or eleven dimensions, not the three (plus Time) that we generally acknowledge. Second, it proves "entanglement" exists.

Radin suggests that we humans likewise operate as bundles of entangled subatomic particles, reaching out and engaging with one another in invisible ways. And it may be so. Except that our atoms and molecules are packed so tightly together that they are anything but unperturbed. They bump into each other all the time. Yet . . . sometimes we have remarkable intuitions!

For millennia, mystics have claimed that all is One, that everything is composed of the *suchness* of God, and that all these heightened sensitivities, intentions and angels, psychic and luminous powers are normal. And now I'll go out on a limb. I think they are carried on ribbons of love.

I mean it literally.

Once my daughter and I were in India visiting my spiritual teacher. When it came time to leave, he escorted us to the bus station, helped us on the bus, and stood back to wave us off. We watched him across the parking lot. Suddenly the bus was surrounded by a crowd: men, women, all shouting, singing, waving their hands high in the air, crying out—a riot? I was startled by the noise, the waving saris, the bare arms, the glowing faces, the outstretched hands, when suddenly I realized they had grouped below *our* window, hands lifted to *us*, my daughter and me, all reaching out in praise and adoration. I looked over at Maharaj beyond the crowd and felt his love pouring out toward us in a golden ribbon: you could have walked on it, and the crowd, ecstatic, was caught in that energy, dragged along like the pull of a comet's tail, captive to his love. A moment later, and the bus moved off. The guru turned away, and instantly the crowd dispersed. I've often wondered, did these people remember that for one mad moment they had stood beneath a bus window shouting and crying out in praise? Were they embarrassed? Did they go home and tell their husbands or daughters, "I did the oddest thing today—"? Did they feel touched by the Divine? Or seen by Divinity? Or did the guru give them the gift of forgetfulness?

RIBBONS OF LOVE. One day when I was just a young mother, I was writing in my home office. Down the corridor my baby, Molly, lay sleeping on a bed barricaded by pillows, though she was still too young to move—she hadn't even tried to roll over yet. I was deep in thought, concentrating on my work, when suddenly I jerked alert: "Molly's falling off the bed!"

I raced down the hallway . . . and caught her in midair. It seems impossible. How did I know she was about to fall? It wasn't telepathy; she'd sent no message. At that age, the baby didn't know what "roll over" was, much less "fall." Premonition? Precognition? What bonds of love so enfold a mother and child (or father and child) that we know what's going to happen even down the hall?

Not only are children the repositories of infinite
possibilities, but they also have within them still the
murmur of angel wings, an essence of divinity, unscathed.
With adults . . . I have often felt unspoken challenge . . .
With children it is different. They believe. They accept.
They do not doubt in the terms of adult doubt. They wait
upon the spirit in the fullness of their child wonder . . .
their innocence opens the gateway of faith—and healing.

AMBROSE WORRALL, healer and aeronautical engineer

How can the mind reach into the future? And if it changes a future event, was it the future anyway? In his book *The Power of Premonitions*, Larry Dossey tells of a mother who woke up from a dream in which the chandelier in the baby's room fell and crushed the infant in its crib. Her husband told her to go back to sleep—it was just a dream—but she was so shaken that she actually got up and brought the baby into bed with her. Later that night they heard the crash as the chandelier fell on the empty crib.

I AM NOT A SCIENTIST, but I am convinced that the greater your empathy and the higher your spiritual development, the more intuitive experiences you will have, until such things become so ordinary that you hardly notice them anymore. No longer rare and dramatic, they fall like soft rain into our lives, brushing aside all logical consciousness.

Yet for many people, our intuitions and precognitions are anything but normal. They usually concern danger either to us or to those we love. Your daughter is in trouble, and you wake up, having seen it in a dream! Your husband has been shot in a distant war, and you feel the bullet enter your own body. You needn't wait for the confirming telegram. We are hooked into life by the mystery of love, as we ourselves are love, our very atoms formed of love, and why should it be otherwise when our very thoughts would merge in love?

Once, while working quietly at my desk, I felt my heart jump, torn by a pain so searing I thought it had split in two. I almost fainted. A moment later I was able to breathe again. I sat there, trembling. Had I had a heart attack? I seemed all right. Should I see a doctor? Reaching out mentally, searching, I came to a man I loved who lived on another continent. Had he been hurt? When I managed to reach him a few days later, I discovered he'd had a heart attack at that time. So intimately were we connected that I think I simultaneously experienced his pain.

What I am going to tell you about is what we teach our physics students in the third or fourth year of graduate school. . . . It is my task to convince you not to turn away because you don't understand it. You see, my physics students don't understand it either. . . . That is because I don't understand it. Nobody does.

NOBEL LAUREATE RICHARD FEYNMAN

I have a friend, Susan, who was engaged to a man she deeply loved. They were waiting only for his divorce to come through to marry. One evening, as he opened the apartment door, she felt a jolt of sheer rage. It shook her to the core as she watched her dog leap joyously toward this man, tail wagging, mouth open, grinning as only dogs can do. "Major!" she shouted at the dog. "Come here!" She pulled the dog off by the collar. She didn't want him even to touch her lover, much less offer welcome. She stood, arms crossed before him, trembling. She knew before he said a word: He was going back to his wife. Oh, they talked that evening. They talked and talked. But what amazed Susan was that she had known with utter certainty, with his hand resting on the outside doorknob, the decision he'd already made.

I remember once turning to an acquaintance and blurting, "Oh, you're going to get married!" The words shot out of my mouth.

"Who told you that?" I thought he was going to hit me.

"No one." I cringed before his wrath. "I'm sorry. Forget it. I don't know why I said that."

But, of course, six weeks later he announced he'd secretly married a woman thirty years younger to whom he'd been engaged eight weeks.

Even those of us who live in cities, who rarely see the moon and stars and don't practice psychic gifts, telepathy, sixth sense, vibes, or extrasensory perception—we too occasionally hear whispers of the Divine . . . and marvel at the implications.

The greater your empathy and the higher your spiritual development, the more intuitive experiences you will have.

"Our lives are like islands in the sea," wrote William James, the philosopher, "or like trees in the forest. The maple and the pine may whisper to each other with their leaves, and . . . [the islands] hear each other's foghorns. But the trees also commingle their roots in the darkness underground, and the islands also hang together through the ocean's bottom: Just so there is a continuum of cosmic consciousness . . . into which our several minds plunge as into a mother-sea or reservoir."

We are islands joined deep beneath the sea, but the wind is also ruffling the shimmering green tips of the trees that rise up high above our loamy shore, making it hard sometimes to read the signals at our roots.

three

STUDIES & SKEPTICS

*It is foolish to be convinced without
evidence, but it is equally foolish to refuse
to be convinced by real evidence.*

UPTON SINCLAIR

HOW OFTEN DO WE have a hunch that we refuse to listen to?
Mary Anne offers one such cautionary tale. She married a man
she was wild about. One month after the wedding, she was making coffee one morning when she felt compelled to open her
husband's suitcase, and saw among the many papers it contained
one envelope that drew her attention. To her surprise she discovered her husband had been stealing money from her to pay for
school tuition that he claimed he'd already paid.

It was a shock, but she refused the information, she says,
"because I loved him so much."

A year later, she was home alone, and again she had an
intuition—an urge, for no conceivable reason, to hit the redial
button on the phone. It rang through to an answering machine
and a woman's voice giving her name and the request to call.

"I was so confused," she wrote. By then she felt physically
guided. "I sat down, and then I sensed another direction to go
look in his car." Since her husband had said he would be at
church, she knew where to find it.

"I'll never forget walking down the street to his car, feeling like a fool but also like a robot being led. I found the car and felt satisfied, but then found myself urged to open the back door and look in a specific area, where I found a letter from the same woman with her name, her phone number, and the keys to her house. I could no longer hide from the facts. I had married a philanderer and a con artist!"

A cynic would sneer that the intuition would have been more useful before she ever married the man. Another might argue that Mary Anne was unconsciously reading subtle signals that set off her suspicions: body language, a tone of voice, too many wrong numbers on the phone, the shrug of a shoulder, a look: nothing paranormal or metaphysical, just plain old ordinary common sense.

But skeptics have their own row to hoe.

IT IS COMMONLY BELIEVED that psychic phenomena cannot be replicated under laboratory conditions and therefore cannot be scientifically demonstrated. It's not true. Scientists have been studying telepathy, intuition, and psychic matters (*psi*) since the early 1800s. The London Society for Psychical Research was founded in 1882 by such scientific luminaries as the physicist Sir Oliver Lodge (known for contributions to wireless telegraphy); Nobel laureate Baron Rayleigh; Samuel P. Langley, secretary of the Smithsonian Institution; psychologist William James; and Edward C. Pickering, director of the Harvard Observatory. The Society does academic research. Two years later, in 1884, the College of Psychic Studies was founded in London to explore and teach a consciousness beyond matter. In 1911 a chair for psychical research at Stanford University was funded, and in the 1930s biologist J. B. Rhine (who coined the term ESP and also

the word *parapsychology*) was in full swing at the famous paranormal research program that he founded at Duke University and
that continued until 1965. It was Rhine, together with Sir Oliver
Lodge in Britain and German colleagues, who developed the
analytical and statistical methods necessary to professionalize
parapsychology research, and Rhine who founded the *Journal
of Parapsychology*. Meanwhile, in 1951, the brilliant medium Ei-
leen Garrett established the Parapsychology Foundation in New
York City.

But the great flourishing of paranormal research came only
toward the end of the twentieth century with the rise of technology and computers. Hundreds of thousands of laboratory studies have now been carried out in such acclaimed institutions as
Harvard University, Princeton, Stanford, the Institute of Noetic
Sciences, and in venues from Scotland to Sweden, Germany to
Australia. They have substantiated the reality of intuition, clairvoyance, telepathy, and precognition. Do we need more proof?
Dean Radin, in his 2006 book *Entangled Minds*, charts the numerous tests that document precognitive dreams, telepathy, intuition, the uneasy sense of being stared at, and remote viewing. He
notes that the studies show odds against such things happening
by chance so astronomical that you can hardly read the figures:
odds of 48 billion to one, or of 1.1 million to one, or of 131 million
to 1^{27} (which is .0000000000000000000000000001, or twenty-
seven zeros before the 1—pretty small). More than one thousand
controlled studies of *psi* have been concluded with combined
odds against chance of 10^{104} to 1.

In one analysis of precognition studies conducted in the fifty
years between 1935 and 1985, two researchers analyzed 309
tests consisting of nearly two million individual trials using over
50,000 subjects. In these "forced-choice" tests a person is asked
to predict which one of a fixed number of possible targets would

be randomly selected *later*. The targets were colored lamps or the face of a tossed die or Zener cards (showing the symbols of a circle, square, cross, triangle, or wavy lines). The time interval between the guesses and the selection of future targets ranged from milliseconds to a year. The results of the 309 studies produced odds against chance of 10^{25} to one, which means the chance that coincidence was involved was 10 million billion billion to one! Ten years later two researchers from the University of Edinburgh published an analysis of forced-choice experiments comparing clairvoyance (perceiving the present) to precognition (perceiving the future) and found twenty-two studies from 1935 to 1997 with odds for clairvoyance of 400 to 1 and of precognition of 1.1 million to 1.

In another highly controlled test on telepathy performed by the Rhine Psychology Lab at Duke University, again using Zener cards, success rates offered odds against chance of 375 trillion to one.

New inventions and technologies have led to increasingly sophisticated tests. We can now measure brain waves, heartbeat, and tiny fluctuations in skin conductance (sweat), and these offer exquisitely sensitive indications of presentiments. In one of my favorites on telepathy, performed at the University of Pennsylvania, a husband and wife were isolated in two separate rooms. While the husband watched a variety of images on a computer, his wife was hooked up to electrodes that measured unconscious physiological responses, including tiny fluctuations in skin galvanization. Among the many images on her husband's computer were photographs of his wife, and each time her picture came on the screen he experienced a wave of pleasure. Remarkably, each time he thought of her, his wife, in the next room, showed tiny changes in skin conductivity, telepathically picking up her husband's warm response.

In another study, this time of precognition, again using electrodes to measure subtle physical changes in the palms of the
hand, researchers devised a test using three kinds of images appearing randomly on a computer screen. The images were either
calm or emotionally charged. The participant presses a button on
the computer when he's ready for the test. Within five seconds
(six seconds in another study) the computer selects a picture at
random from a pool of images, displays it for three seconds, and
goes blank. After ten seconds a message appears telling the subject to press the screen again when he's ready for the next picture.
The idea behind these tests is that we are constantly and unconsciously scanning the future and preparing to respond to it, and
that the body responds in direct proportion to the (future) emotional impact: it's the gift of fear, it's the gift of fear we're speaking
of. A poisonous spider is something to be concerned about, and
the woman who intuitively withdraws her hand from the wood-
pile for no apparent reason may be the one who survives.

Participants reacted with changes in skin conductivity two to
three seconds *before* the violent images, as might be expected,
while calm or neutral pictures produced small or no results. But
on average the subjects anticipated an extremely emotional future situation *by three seconds*. In this study the odds against
chance were 500 to 1.

A human anticipates a future event by three seconds.
An earthworm has a one-second precognitive response.
Earthworms travel in herds.

We know, however, that intuition can occur far in advance
of three small seconds. Mishkat Al Moumin, a divorced Iraqi

woman (and anyone familiar with Muslim culture knows the degradation that divorce incurs), a lawyer and Ph.D., was minister of the environment during Ayad Allawi's 2004–2005 term as prime minister. She believed that "environment" meant clean drinking water for families, functioning sewer lines, the ability to find food and cooking oil, and even human rights for women. When a *fatwa* was issued calling for her death, she eventually left Iraq and works now for her country in the United States. But the story I want to tell happened when she was still in Iraq, a minister of the fledgling government.

Beautiful, with short hennaed hair, a round face, and intelligent eyes, Mishkat is a woman of enormous willpower and energy. One night, she dreamed that she was being hunted by men with rifles who were intent on killing her. That morning she could barely drag herself to work. Every movement was slow. Usually she was gone by eight in the morning, but on this day it was eight-thirty before she stepped reluctantly out her door, unable to shake her lassitude, her uncharacteristic lethargy—or the dark sense that *something was wrong*.

Mishkat drove to her office with her bodyguards in a three-car caravan designed to blend into normal traffic: the first car, white, was a small two-door vehicle containing three men. Her four-door yellow auto held the driver and a bodyguard in the front seat and herself in the back, where a woman should sit when driven by her brother or father in a Muslim country. The last car, a black van, trailing unobtrusively by fifty meters, held four more bodyguards.

They drove down a narrow street. Mishkat was engrossed, reading files, when suddenly her car swerved to the right and careened up onto the sidewalk, followed immediately by an explosion as the car behind blew up, killing all her guards. A sui-

cide driver had tried to ram her car, missed, and hit the following
vehicle!

She was devastated. Grieving for her men. But looking back,
she wondered if she'd had an intuition that morning, had tried
intuitively to change the situation—albeit unsuccessfully—by
being late. Later she decided that a scout must have been posted
outside her apartment to telephone the suicide bomber the moment she reached her car, for how else could they have orchestrated the attack?

IN 2004, psychophysiologist Rollin McCraty and his colleagues
reported in the *Journal of Alternative and Complementary Medicine* on their experiments in determining *where* in the brain or
body intuition lies. Their measurements included skin conductance, heart rate, and brain measurements. Replicating the earlier study, thirty calm and fifteen emotionally arousing pictures
were presented to twenty-six participants. It was found that the
heart rate significantly *slowed down* before a future emotional
picture; that while both the heart and brain receive and respond
to intuitive information, the heart appears to receive intuitive
information *before* the brain; that the brain responds in different
ways to calm or to emotionally charged stimuli; and that women
are more attuned than men to intuitive information from the
heart. Is intuition found, then, in the heart?

"The heart," wrote McCraty, "appears to play a direct role in
the perception of future events." In a personal e-mail to me, he
continued: "What our studies suggest is that the heart is the
main conduit that connects us to our higher self or spirit (whatever you want to call it), and that it is the heart that relays intuitive information to the brain, where we may become aware of

it. After the leap of the heart, multiple sites in the brain show pre-stimulus responses, and I suspect the centers involved depend on the type of information passed along (visual, auditory, etc.). But the primary center in the brain appears to be the frontal cortex."

His studies showed the heart slowing down, but I'm reminded of my experiences when playing chess—the pounding heart, the spots before my eyes—that came seconds before I blundered into a mistake.

Sixty percent of adult Americans believe in intuition, clairvoyance, and ESP. Ninety-six percent of scientists from the National Academy of Sciences claim to be skeptics, though 10 percent of them think that parapsychological research should be encouraged.

I'll tell of one last test on intuition. In this study ten adult volunteers were hooked up to a functional magnetic resonance imaging (fMRI) system to measure the oxygen in their blood, on the theory that the higher the oxygen level in one part of the brain, the more likely that that area is being stimulated. (The acronym BOLD means "blood oxygenation level dependent.") Again the participants were asked to look at three kinds of computer-projected images: erotic, violent, and calm or neutral. Each image appeared on the screen for 4.2 seconds, with a blank screen for 8.4 seconds. The results showed that presentiment was distributed throughout the brain, but significant stimulation appeared in one common area.

Men and women showed vast differences. Just before an erotic image appeared on the screen, the men experienced sharp premonitions, but for neutral and violent images they showed nothing. The women, on the other hand, had significant intuitions of both erotic and violent images. Is this why men (some men) find violence less disturbing than women (some women)? Why some even seek out violent adventure in films or games or dangerous sports? The important fact is that the brains of males lit up before an erotic image even appeared, while those of females did so for both erotic and violent ones—and this though neither knew which picture was about to come on screen. Unconsciously, then, we dip into the future—*perceive* it—and God knows how important this is if you're about to step on a snake.

In spite of the research, skepticism runs high in the scientific community. Reputations are at stake, and there is something a little shady and disreputable about investigating hunches, intuition, premonitions, telepathy, and psychic divination. Intellects revolt. But worse is the circular logic that prevails in scientific circles. Research on a topic cannot be taken seriously until it is reported in the "respectable" journals—and it won't be reported until it is considered "respectable."

It is a scandal that the dispute as to the reality of these [psi] phenomena should still be going on, that so many competent witnesses should have declared their belief in them, that so many others should be profoundly interested in having the question determined, and yet, the educated world, as a body, should still be simply in the attitude of incredulity.

HENRY SIDGWICK, Cambridge professor of ethics and
moral philosophy, 1882

Moreover, two curious problems arise concerning studies of intuition and *psi*. First, the more the test is repeated, the worse the perceiver gets. Effects decline. Is that because the human mind revolts in boredom at the endless repetition, or is it because the laboratory setting doesn't really matter anyway; your life is not at stake? Either way, this feeds the disbelief of skeptics.

A second factor is the "Experimenter Effect," whereby the degree of the observer's disdain appears to affect the outcome. "Believe and all things are possible," Jesus Christ admonished. Disbelieve and the study cannot be replicated, as if the mental state of the scientist corrupts the material. Later, we'll see that the trust or skepticism of a client also affects a psychic who is giving a reading, and this should come as no surprise. Have you never found yourself struck speechless before a hostile or contemptuous audience, unable to express yourself? We're all affected by what goes on around us. A flighty horse is panicked by its terrified rider, picking up her fear. A dog senses when you are sad or angry. In the world of subatomic particles, the photon seems almost to adjust to the observer's will, functioning either as a wave or particle, a phenomenon addressed in 1927 by Heisenberg's uncertainty principle, in which he stated that the act of observation itself interferes with the location and velocity of electrons. (This is because observation requires light, and light has momentum.) Why shouldn't the attitude of the investigator, then, affect the studies of higher perception or intuition?

Observer and object are intimately connected. A stream of photons is shot at a screen with two tiny slits in it, while a sensitive camera records where each photon lands. (To me, the first marvel is the camera!) If one of the slits is closed, the photons move single-file like bullets through the single slit. If both slits are open, they meander through the two openings in varying bands of intensity, consistent with a wave.

Oddly, a photon acts as a wave when the scientists aren't looking and like a particle when they are! What makes them collapse into particles when observed?

If you close one slit *after* the photon has already passed through, the photon is seen to have behaved appropriately as a particle; and if you open both slits, then judiciously as a wave. Yet the slits were opened or closed only *after the photon had already passed through!* How could the photon know after it had passed through the slits that one slit would later be shut? In other words, the physicist's choice appears to determine the behavior of the photon. Is reality created by *intention?* Our Free Will?

Nothing is static. Nothing is set. In place of locality, in which objects remain fixed in space and time, *nonlocality* is the operating force; in place of causality, in which everything is clearly caused by an earlier condition (time moving only forward), events are apparently influenced by *intention*; instead of continuity, which assumes no tears in the fabric of time and space, we find *discontinuous* reality, where isolated objects are connected across space and time. Where we once thought things progressed in orderly and predicable ways, we find only chaos and questions, for all our assumptions of reality have been destroyed.

> *[Parapsychology today] is so improbable that extremely good evidence is needed to make us believe it; and this evidence is not good, for how can you trust people who believe in such absurdities?*
>
> EDMUND GURNEY, writing in the 1880s

OUR MINDS ARE AT WAR: intellect and intuition are enemies. The Greek word *skepsis* means "examination" and "doubt," however, not "denial," and current scientific antipathy becomes ludicrous at times, wrote one engineering school authority: "It's the kind of thing I wouldn't believe, even if it were true."

Doubt is our natural state and denial the human response to the unacceptable. It's not surprising then that studies of intuition and presentiment are still woefully inadequate.

"If we imagined [as on a clock] that all funds raised for cancer research were spent in a single day," wrote Dean Radin, "then the comparative funding for psi research—all of it, worldwide, throughout history—is conservatively equivalent to what cancer research consumes in a mere 43 seconds. From this perspective, it's amazing we've learned anything at all. . . ."

Yet look at the studies. The fact is, we know a great deal about intuition and *psi*. How can scientists ignore this inner wisdom?

Experimental Class	Studies	Trials	Odds Against Chance
Dreaming *psi*	47	1,270 sessions	2.2×10^{10} to 1
Ganzfield (telepathy) *psi*	88	3,145 sessions	3.0×10^{19} to 1
Conscious detection of being stared at	65	34,097 sessions	8.5×10^{46} to 1
Unconscious detection of being stared at	15	379 sessions	100 to 1
Unconscious detection of distant intention	40	1,055 sessions	1,000 to 1
Dice PK	169	2.6 million tosses	2.6×10^{76} to 1
RNG PK	595	1.1 billion random events	3,052 to 1
Combined	1,019		1.3×10^{104} to 1

A Meta-Meta-Analysis of Experiments in *Psi* Proving That Outcomes Are Definitely Not Due to Chance[*]

The number of studies listed and the odds against chance are adjusted for potential selective reporting biases using the trim and fill algorithm. Combined results indicate that these experimental results are unlikely to be due to coincidence or dumb luck.

> *The most exciting pharse to hear in science, the one that heralds new discoveries, is not "Eureka!" but "That's funny."*
>
> ISAAC ASIMOV

[*] From Dean Radin, *Entangled Minds: Extrasensory Experiences in a Quantum Reality* (New York: Paraview Pocket Books, 2006), p. 276.

four

THE NATURAL INTUITIVE

*Nothing influences our conduct less than
do intellectual ideas.*

CARL JUNG

INTUITION: you can't touch it or see it or find it on the Internet.
I believe it is our subconscious mind speaking to us from dark
and covert caves. If we do not listen, it will try to send its messages in dreams. Or else it becomes so insistent that we hear it
even as an External Voice. Perhaps it is only our inner selves
talking to ourselves, but sometimes it feels so different, so "oth-
erworldly," that you'd think it could be orchestrated by angels.
Well, why not? Aren't we part of the spiritual dimension? Aren't
we angels at times, acting on behalf of others and being moved
occasionally (to our surprise) in mysterious ways—and always
(how curious) to help another, even when we don't know the
other person is in need of help?

I heard of a woman who one day had the idea she should take
some flowers to the old lady next door. When she knocked, she
found the woman in tears. "I was just praying to God to send
someone," she said. "I felt so lonely. And now you're here."

Scientists proffer seven main theories to explain these heightened perceptions, each an appropriately academic mouthful: We
have signal-transfer theory, goal-oriented theory, field theory, skep-

tical theory, collective-mind theory, multidimensional space/time theory, and quantum-mechanical theory, which is itself composed of five theorettes, one being the aforementioned concept of entangled minds. All this in addition to morphic fields, nonlocality, and thin-slicing of the brain. And still, no one has any idea what's actually going on.

Intuition is some kind of swift intelligence that operates differently from logic, analysis, ratiocination. It is fragile, easily ignored, often overruled by critical doubt. It dislikes being poked and bullied by conscious reason. It has nothing to do with smarts. Oliver Wendell Holmes said of Franklin Delano Roosevelt that he was a second-rate intellect but had first-rate intuition.

Eighty-nine percent of women and seventy-two percent of men report having gut feelings about people or events. Seventy-eight percent of skeptics report gut feelings in which their stomachs felt tied in knots.

Some people have natural psychic gifts, just as some are more mathematically inclined than others. They are by nature open, willing, creative, and adventurous. Doesn't every artist feel lifted sometimes by the Muse and carried effortlessly down that river of creativity, drawn hour after hour by the tide of the work and every word or note near perfect? We think of Mozart writing his symphonies *vertically* bar by bar across the pages, setting down the notes of all the instruments at once, as if he were hearing music dictated to him. Or of Saint Teresa of Ávila, who was once seen praying over her work as her feather dipped itself in ink and wrote without her hand. (Was it merely metaphor?) We marvel at the paintings that appeared mysteriously day after day at Lily Dale, the famous psychic community in upstate New York, while people gathered to watch the forms emerge on the canvas as if the magic brush of a Disney cartoon were pouring out color without a guiding hand.

What in God's name is going on?

SKEPTICS WILL TELL YOU that what's going on is a general decline in scientific education, the deplorable state of present-day unquestioning intellect. The National Science Foundation, in a periodic report entitled *Science and Technology Indicators,* which reviews the public understanding of science, found to its dismay a "widespread and growing" problem of belief in "pseudoscience." A 2001 nationwide poll found that 60 percent of adult Americans believe that "some people possess psychic powers or ESP." When the respondents were separated by education, however, it was found to the horror of some that the higher the education, the more prevalent the belief, with 62 percent of those with high school degrees or higher in agreement! Belief in extrasensory perception in the United States, therefore, is not equated with ignorance and lack of education, *and this is true worldwide,* from Australia to Brazil. In Sweden, with its high literacy rate, the majority of the population believes in the paranormal.

It's enough to drive a skeptic mad.

There is absolutely no reason to suppose that telepathy is anything more than a charlatan's fantasy.

PROFESSOR PETER ATKINS, a chemist at Oxford University who later admitted he had not studied any of the evidence and neither did he feel obliged to do so, as quoted in 2006 in the London *Times*

A PROFILE

Let's cut to the chase: Studies show that people who believe in heightened awareness are not weak-minded, mentally ill, or lacking in critical faculties. They are not ignorant and uneducated. Nor are they superstitious, holding with outdated beliefs in witchcraft or demons or matters cabalistic and occult. It's not that their brains are misfiring or subject to schizophrenic seizures, although both spiritual and psychic experiences are *correlated* with increased brain activity.

Creative and high-achieving people report more psychic experiences than those whose creativity has been choked off.

Well, then, who has these experiences? In 2003, at a conference at the Institute of Noetic Sciences, 465 people were asked about their education, allergies and bodily sensitivities, mental practices (such as meditation), and *psi* experiences. It was found that women reported more experiences than men and younger people more than older; that left-handed and ambidextrous individuals were significantly more likely to have experiences than right-handed ones; and that those who were psychic had a clear pattern of allergies and bodily sensitivities. Fifty percent of women were *un*telepathic, but 85 percent of the telepaths were female. They are younger, educated, and creative, with abilities of association and absorption. They have high focus or concentration.

A profile of a psychic would be: a left-handed, somewhat introverted, creative woman about age thirty or younger who is physically sensitive (perhaps with allergies), suffers perhaps from chronic anxiety, makes decisions based on emotion rather than logic, practices a mental discipline such as meditation, and is open, willing, courageous, unconventional, and curious. It's interesting that creative and high-achieving people report more psychic experiences than those whose creativity has been stifled by social conditioning and inhibitions.

Studies show that ESP is associated with a relaxed state of mind and an unrestricted level of consciousness.

THE MYERS-BRIGGS TEST

I believe that everyone has intuition and moreover that it can be developed. But there's no question some people have it to a higher degree than others. To the extreme intuitive, the psychic who listens to directions from a Higher Source or Self, it seems that everyone would have these abilities. I brought this up to a board member of the Society for Psychical Research in London. He looked at me in surprise and answered no. He had never had a psychic experience in his life, which didn't mean that he wasn't fascinated by the subject. Which is why he served on the Society board.

It was the famous Swiss psychologist C. G. Jung who developed the theory of differing personality types, depending on how people *perceive* the world and how they *respond* to it. He proposed the existence of two ways of thinking: the rational (judging) functions, which include thinking and sensing; and the irrational (perceiving) functions, including sensing and intuition. Isabel Briggs Myers and her mother, Katharine Cook Briggs, took Jung's idea and in the 1940s developed a series of psychological tests to provide an indicator for sixteen possible character traits that form our personality preferences. Since then millions have taken the Myers-Briggs Type Indicator tests, answering pages of seemingly unrelated questions and in the process discovering their own strengths and weaknesses—often with relief that *it's okay to be me!*

The first series of questions determine whether you are an *extrovert* or an *introvert*. How do you engage the outer world? Do you restore your batteries in a social setting, or do you need long periods of silence, solitude? There's an old joke: How to the extrovert "hell at a party" means "not getting in," while to the introvert hell is "being there." The extrovert is focused on the external world and social intercourse, the introvert on some deep inner communion. The one is often concerned with action, the other with the search for deep truths.

The second indicator refers to two distinct and contrasting ways of perceiving the world. How do you acquire information, through your five *senses* or by some inexplicable *intuition*? Those who prefer to rely on their senses may be so attuned to the physical world that they little heed the faint nudges of wisdom coming out of nowhere, the whispers of the heart.

The third series of questions reveal how a person processes information: by *thinking* in an analytical and logical fashion or by subjective *feelings*.

The fourth and last tests determine a person's dominant mode of dealing with the external world: is she a "perceiver," as they call it, studying and acquiring information with appropriate revision of one's worldview, or, at the opposite pole, a "judging" type, coming quickly to decisions, reaching a verdict. To this latter personality type, the "judging" type, it almost doesn't matter *what* decision is made as long as one is made! To the "perceiver," reaching a conclusion is seen as eliminating options. It's a denial of life itself! To the judging type, the hesitation and equivocation of the "perceiver," who is always ready to change his mind, is anathema!

Each of these four inborn preferences, or personality traits, lies in opposition to its subordinate or auxiliary trait, so that all possible indicators combine to create the unique and individual *you*. You may be an Introverted iNtuitive Feeling Perceiving (INFP), an Extroverted Sensing Thinking Judging (ESTJ), an Introverted Sensing Thinking Perceiving (ISTP), or any one of sixteen combinations. The dominant characteristics are only preferences, however, and a sensing type, for example, may tilt only slightly to that method of acquiring information, while also displaying a high degree of intuition. Moreover, as we mature, our childhood subordinate or auxiliary attribute *is supposed to* strengthen and balance out the dominant traits, until we have the ability to utilize all possible eight characteristics and with practice gain access to all qualities. You may be exceptionally intuitive as a child and prefer this method of receiving information, but it doesn't mean you can't train yourself to become aware of the sensory world around you. You may be an extrovert by nature but learn to enjoy solitude to such an extent that your introversion becomes almost as important.

For the highly social activist who receives information principally through his five senses, analyzes it by ratiocination, and lays claim to decisive closure, the difficulty may be the same as that of the dreamy, sensitive, intuitive type: He can't imagine operating any other way. Of *course* he condemns those with intuitive or extrasensory heightened perceptions. He deems them charlatans, irresponsible, embarrassments to scientific inquiry.

The idea of trusting the still, small, fragile whispers of intuition is for him improbable. And yet he, too, has intuitions and psychic experiences, and these come at him with exceptional and dramatic force, for how else could he be made aware of them?

I know a woman who says she has no intuition. She doesn't miss it. She makes up for it with her intellectual brilliance and energy. I think she must be ESTJ. There are also those unfortunates who may have been scorched by disease, mind-addling addictions, or mental disorders, leaving their intuition impaired, but even these individuals can develop true intuition as they heal.

Then, too, there are some who mistrust these inner nudges, because of the troubling questions they raise: "How do I know my intuition comes from God?" they ask, dismissing the illusion of guidance as a form of dangerous egotism that threatens to lunge down a false path, carrying the whole family over the cliff.

As you grow sensitive to the ways that you receive intuition, you will observe that it is always on your side. Your intuition solves a problem, or it saves your life. It comes often as an inner warning, and later, as you become increasingly attuned, you notice it surrounds you constantly, offering little gifts and blessings. Soon you can't tell the difference between intuition and simply getting on with life.

If, however, you have an urge to kill your wife, to steal, to defraud or oppress another, to create havoc by sexual misconduct or addiction, or if you are possessed by hatred and a desire for revenge, you may be certain this is not true "intuition." I think that these hungers come from the darker side of our souls, asking not to be acted on but to be noticed in order to be healed.

An intuition is swift and fleeting. The urge to do harm, on the other hand, may be so intense and linger so long that you may even act on it. Moreover, you will feel aftereffects, both thrilling and disgusting, and the distaste has its own allure.

True intuition, frail, fragile, sensitive, elusive, never comes like that. It never harms.

Inviting Intuition I: Relaxed & Easy

Intuition is not reached through the conscious or thinking mind, which locks onto intellect, logic, and analysis. It is seen with the inarticulate dream-mind, the subconscious or unconscious. Please note, I'm using the words not in the classical model of *ego, id,* and *superego* as defined by Sigmund Freud but in the loose sense of the artist's inventive mind: that part of the brain that we use when daydreaming, or sleeping, or weeding the garden mindlessly, or meditating, or absorbed in creating a painting, music, or other work of art.

For intuition, you need the simplicity of the child-mind, the dreaming mind that tosses out images and information when you are asleep. I think it's important to encourage your children, therefore, to daydream, space out, go woolgathering. We don't need to fill every moment of their days with activities. Let them learn to be alone, and the same holds true for adults too.

You need to be comfortable with silence and solitude. Learn to be quiet. Turn off the TV. Shut down the computer and video games. Befriend yourself. "Go watch the grass grow," as my mother used to say. "Do nothing." And you'll be amazed how much is revealed to you by merely opening yourself to your environment, observing with attention and without judgment.

Allow yourself to dream. Your Higher Consciousness will point out where you ought to go.

five

INSPIRATION & CREATIVITY

The two Brontës, Emily and Charlotte—
where did they get their wildness? And
Tolstoy at times—how did he ever come at
the inwardness of being a prisoner on the
long French retreat from Moscow? . . .
Where does the music come from that
composers hear in their inward ears?

MARY C. MORRISON

IS INSPIRATION, IS CREATIVITY ITSELF, an aspect of intuition? We know that inspiration, like intuition, strikes when you are relaxed and in a quiet, receptive mental state. Perhaps you've worked like a demon for days (and working flat-out is one of the requirements) until, exhausted, you give up. You drag yourself to bed. In sleep the answer comes, drifting up from the unconscious and handed to you like the apple in Eden. Isn't this why writers and composers keep paper and pencil by their beds, knowing that inspiration strikes in that hazy half-sleeping state when your brain has access to your unconscious, the inner problem solver? Just as meditation offers peace and serenity, it also sharpens intuition. You sit down to meditate. Relax. Soften your tongue. Focus on your breath. You observe the thoughts that move like clouds across the sky of your awareness, drifting in and out, and sometimes, unaware, you discover yourself caught up in creative inspiration beyond your wildest dreams. You don't need to sit cross-legged before an altar like a monk, though that practice is not to be sneezed at. Your meditation may consist of a walk in the woods, the steady raking of autumn leaves, trimming the hedges—anything that pulls you away from your immediate problems, puts you outdoors, and allows the mind to relax. There's a reason Buddhists call meditation the "wish-fulfilling tree." Your dreams come true as you practice meditating.

I've never invented anything, but once while meditating at a Vipassana Buddhist retreat (they don't call it "insight meditation" for nothing), I "saw" the way a table is composed of atoms and the way the atoms danced. But how could I "see" an effect that can't even be viewed under a microscope?

The insight was not new. The Greek philosopher and geometer Democritus of Abdera (460–370 BC) proposed the existence of an ultimate particle that he called *atomos*. Indeed, the idea goes back even further, to his teacher Leucippus. Aristotle disdained the idea, but by the first century BC the theory of atoms was so widely accepted that Roman writer Lucretius mentioned atoms in his two-hundred-page poem *De Rerum Natura* (*On the Nature of Things*), in which he spoke of "assemblies" of very small building blocks that collided and fell apart as they formed the material world.

> . . . *no respite's ever given*
> *To atoms through the fathomless void but, rather, they are driven*
> *By sundry restless motions. After colliding, some will leap*
> *Great intervals apart, while others harried by blows will keep*
> *In a narrow space. Those atoms that are bound together tight,*

When they collide with something, their recoil is only
slight
Since they are tangled up in their own intricate
formation:
Such are the particles that form the sturdy roots of stone,
And make up savage iron and other substances of this kind.

Lucretius was an Epicurean philosopher who believed that things are exactly what they seem to be: Our senses don't deceive us. Had Lucretius viewed this phenomenon himself by inspiration, insight, or clairvoyance? Had he seen it while in meditation?

Perhaps a more striking example of psychic inspiration is the case of Annie Besant and Charles Leadbeater, the British theosophists who described in their 1908 book, *Occult Chemistry,* a clairvoyant vision of the internal structure of atoms, including a new form of the element neon, which they called a *meta-neon,* and claimed it to have an atomic weight of 22.33. Francis Aston, then a physics assistant to Sir J. J. Thomson at Cambridge University in England (the man who identified the electron in the atom), had read *Occult Chemistry* before discovering in 1912, while analyzing neon gas, a substance with that same atomic weight of 22.33. His discovery became a key to the development of the atomic bomb. In 1922 Aston received the Nobel Prize, and such is the distaste of scientists for psychic phenomena and intuition that curiously he neglected to credit in his acceptance speech the inspiration of theosophist clairvoyance.

Creative people report more psychic experiences, see farther into the depths of the world, than other people do.

But what exactly is inspiring us? Is it simply our unconscious mind awakening and spewing out information lodged in forgotten memories or making connections we hadn't recognized before? The verb *inspire* derives from the Latin word meaning "to breathe in." Subtly enfolded in its essence is the sense that something is breathing into us, as God breathed into the clay of Adam to fill him with life.

Some people—Dante, Shakespeare, Schiller, Goethe, Bach, Beethoven, and hosts of modern artists—demonstrate extraordinary creativity. Likewise scientists, inventors, engineers, mathematicians, cooks. According to the neuroscientist and psychiatrist Nancy C. Andreasen, in her book *The Creative Brain: the Science of Genius*, the brains of such giants differ qualitatively from those of ordinary people. Their thought and neural processes are different, she says (though how she would know, since they're dead, remains a mystery). What is interesting is that creative people seem to *listen* in the same way that people with psychic abilities do.

"I slip into a state," writes the playwright Neil Simon, "that is apart from reality. . . . I don't write consciously—it is as if the muse sits on my shoulder."

The same thing happens when you move into the intuitive mind, the state where the paranormal may also come into play. You go into a slightly altered state. You turn off the churning thoughts of everyday banking and bruising. You allow yourself to be still. Listening. Often this mindless state is achieved by quiet, repetitive motions: taking a walk, knitting, cleaning, cooking, ironing, weeding the garden, repairing the roof, sanding your boat. Slowly you enter the restful quietude of "no-mind." Often a rocking sensation helps, as when traveling in a train or bus, in which the gentle soothing motion somehow swings you into that receptive childlike part of the brain, where you can be taken over by your Higher Self.

"When I am, as it were, completely in myself, entirely alone, and of good cheer," wrote Mozart, "say, traveling in a carriage, or walking after a good meal, or during the night when I cannot sleep; it is on such occasions that my ideas flow best and most abundantly. Whence and how they come, I know not; nor can I force them . . . Nor do I hear in my imagination the parts successively, but I hear them, as it were, all at once. What a delight this is I cannot tell!"

Sometimes you are given no more than a fragment of the work before the Muse, distracted, turns away, the spigot shuts off, and then, using your own small, pitiful, human resources, you wrestle with the work, tussling and struggling to beat the material into shape; or else you strain to hear the distant echoes of inspiration, like fairy bells, too faint for even the most sensitive ear. The creative process is different from conscious analytic thought. Ideas collide in a dreamlike state or else rise up like bubbles in that hypnagogic state you occupy just as you are drifting into sleep.

Here is Tchaikovsky, speaking of his musical inspiration.

Generally speaking, the germ of a future composition comes suddenly and unexpectedly. If the soul is ready—that is to say, if the disposition for work is there—it takes root with extraordinary force and rapidity, shoots up through the earth, puts forth branches, leaves, and finally, blossoms. I cannot define the creative process in any other way. . . .

In the summer of 1741, George Frideric Handel composed his famous oratorio *Messiah* in a single burst of exalted inspiration. It took twenty-seven days, less than a month, and the music carried him to heights of ecstasy. One day his assistant found the composer with tears running down his cheeks. Handel held up the score to the "Hallelujah Chorus": "I think I have seen the face of God," he said.

Artists, writers, and musicians are not the only people who are struck by inspiration. Was this the state of Archimedes when he solved the problem of how to determine whether an irregularly shaped crown was made of alloy or of gold? He was still puzzling over the question when, stepping into his bath, he noticed the water level rise and understood in a flash of inspiration that the volume of water displaced was equal to the volume of that portion of his body in the water. Thus he could calculate with precision the volume of an irregular object. He was so excited that he leaped from the tub and ran naked down the streets of Syracuse, shouting *Eureka!* Which translates roughly as "I've got it!"

But where did it come from, his bolt from the blue? It is an axiom that solutions present themselves only after hard, grinding work followed by release. I know one mathematician who in the act of lovemaking suddenly stopped ("Wait! Wait!"), reached for his pen, and began to scribble down the solution that his subconscious mind presented at that moment of climactic exuberance. It's in the restful state, usually, however, as you drop off to sleep, or soak in a bath, or take a walk, that answers float unbidden to the surface of your consciousness. Inspiration. Handed you by God.

> *If automatic writing appears under the flag of the unleashed subconscious, actualizing itself outside volition . . . , it also proclaims the poet's innocent wish to force inspiration.*
>
> ODYSSEUS ELYTIS, Nobel laureate

PARACELSUS WAS A PHYSICIAN and alchemist who applied his knowledge of chemistry to the healing arts. He wrote dozens of scientific works, including *Der Grossen Wundartzney* (*Great Surgery Book*) and made groundbreaking advances in treating disease and wounds. He died in 1541 at the age of forty-eight, wealthy and renowned. "That which the dream shows," he wrote, "is the shadow of such wisdom as exists in man, even if during his waking state he may know nothing about it. . . . We do not know it because we are fooling away our time with outward and perishing things, and are asleep in regard to that which is real within ourselves."

Which mathematician was it (do you know?) whose wife would dream of mathematical solutions? I heard that her husband kept paper and pencil by his bedside so that when his wife awoke he could write down what she'd seen, for she knew nothing about mathematics or the meaning of what she dreamed.

Another example of the creativity of dreams came in the late nineteenth century, when the German chemist Friedrich August Kekulé von Stradonitz dreamed he saw a snake eating its own tail, which gave the appearance of a large ring. At the time von Stradonitz was engaged in research on the six carbon atoms in the molecule of benzene, which he envisioned as a straight line. On waking from his dream he realized that in fact they form a *ring*. His discovery is regarded as one of the greatest flashes of creative genius in the entire field of organic chemistry.

Intuition or not, however, the recipient must be not only aware and awake but also ready to receive. Nothing will persuade me that the author of those poems and plays, the man who gave us such women as Portia, Rosalind, Lady Macbeth, Gertrude, Ophelia, Desdemona, Cordelia, Goneril, Regan; a man who clearly had traveled widely, read copiously, and was conversant with the Bible, royal politics, aristocratic ways, the culture of the court, and the history and literature of his time; a man who, at a minimum, spoke English and French (but likely also Latin, Italian, Greek, and a smattering of other languages), was a commoner, the father of two illiterate daughters; a man whose will mentions no writings or plays and no books (expensive, leather-bound), whose tomb was dignified with a self-penned piece of pathetic doggerel, and whose neighbors were unaware of his having composed immortal plays. Even if Creativity is the handmaid of Intuition, even if angels are dictating from some Higher Dimension, the vessel or conduit for this work (the artist) must have the vocabulary and experience to transcribe what he hears. Mozart was the son of a musician, as were the sons of Johann Sebastian Bach, and Bach himself, and Beethoven and Mendelssohn. True, Schubert was the son of Moravian peasants, but he had intense musical training beginning at the age of five. The creative artist does not work in a vacuum of intuitive genius; he is grounded in the craft. His duty is to get so fine an education, to be so versed in the chosen science or craft in which he works, that Intuition and Inspiration may plant their foothold in his heart.

THE WRITER C. M. MAYO told me that once when writing her novel *The Last Prince of the Mexican Empire* she came to a section and was utterly blocked. She couldn't write. One character eluded her, and she couldn't proceed until she found the clue to his nature. Finally, in desperation, she called a psychic, an intuitive or "sensitive," who went into a slightly altered state and began to speak about the fictional character of her historical novel. She gave Catherine a visual image for him that bumped her back into writing.

Where do the thoughts come from that invade my mind? It's so mysterious. Every writer knows this sensation of not being completely in control. The way a character comes knocking at the doors of consciousness, stalks into the living room, and settles by the fire without a by-your-leave, insists on smoking against your will (what is a cheroot anyway?), knocking the ashes on your rug until you're finally forced to stop your plans for the book and give him your attention. Perhaps he's only a minor character, but you both know (he strutting and arrogant, and you by now resigned) that now he's going to steal each scene.

> *He who is born in imagination discovers the latent forces of Nature. . . . Besides the stars that are established, there is yet another—Imagination—that begets a new star and a new heaven.*
>
> PARACELSUS

I know another writer who sometimes sets down a word she doesn't even know. *Where did that word come from?* she thinks as she lurches to the dictionary, only to find that it carries exactly the connotation she wants. She laughs that she has a scholar guide who helps her even when she doesn't think to ask. He has a better vocabulary than she.

But what artist hasn't had such experiences? I remember puttering along on one "omniscient author" novel when suddenly a first-person narrator popped up, bringing me to a full stop. For months I could not proceed. He refused to move off, and I refused to let him in. Finally, defeated, I decided to plow ahead, to trust: I could always go back later (I consoled myself) and remove him from the book, and since I couldn't write without him, I might as well see what he had to say. Throughout, he surprised me with his unanticipated twists. When I came to the end of the book I realized the novel was far better for being told by him. But where had he come from? Inspiration? Our Higher Selves, our guides and angels, know far more than we.

THE EXTERNAL VOICE

Occasionally this inspiration is so strong, it comes as an External Voice. The phenomenon is so commonplace that it appears in literature around the world. In his short story "Old-fashioned Farmers," Nikolai Gogol wrote: "It has doubtless happened to you, at some time or other, to hear a voice calling you by name." The narrator adds that he has heard the voice many times in his childhood. "I confess . . . " he continues, "that it was very terrifying to *me*," frightening because the Russian peasants believed an external voice to be the man's spirit longing for him and calling him to death. In Charlotte Brontë's *Jane Eyre*, when Jane is about to go to India with St. John Rivers, she hears Rochester calling her name aloud, and so clear is it that she refuses River and travels back to Thornfield Hall and the man she loves.

I heard of a *National Geographic* photographer who wanted his work published. Walking one day in Hawaii, dejected and forlorn, he heard a voice speak to him aloud: "Go see XYZ."

He looked around, surprised. Where had that voice come from? He didn't know the man the voice suggested, indeed had never heard the name before. He went home and asked his sister if she'd ever heard of anyone with that name. She did. That man became his publisher.

Joan of Arc heard voices, and mystics sometimes attest to the external direction. It's called clairaudience.

One day Saint Augustine (not yet a saint) was praying in his garden. At the time he was filled with doubt and self-loathing. He twisted in the chains of his despair, unable to dedicate himself to God and to the life of chastity that he felt the move required, and yet unable to continue living lustily as before. He threw himself on the ground, tears streaming down his face, then heard a child's voice: *"Sume, lege!"* it called. "Pick it up. Read!" He reached for the book beside him, which happened to be the *Epistles* of Saint Paul, read the first words his eyes fell on, and in one instant was converted in an excess of grace and joy. He had no difficulty giving up his mistress, for suddenly he burned heart and soul for God.

Usually the Voice has lesser things to say. One time when I was in Italy, I was on my way to meet friends in Lucca, but I had managed to catch the wrong train and ended up late at night in the wrong town. Unable to call my friends (this was before cell phones), I checked into the railroad station hotel and fell into exhausted sleep, only to be woken the next morning by my mother calling me by my nickname: "Penny! Penny! Wake up! Hurry! You have to hurry!" I scrambled up. My mother had been dead for years, but I never doubted it was she. I threw on clothes, grabbed a taxi to Lucca, and found my friends about to leave for the weekend. They'd given up on me.

Not long ago I was talking to a State Department officer who told me that after his mother died she had woken him up on several occasions, always with her own voice pulling him out of sleep. Once she told him to put iodine on his bad case of poison ivy. It worked.

Years ago I received a letter from a woman in New Jersey who wrote of how, soon after she had first married, her husband left her for his girlfriend. She was devastated, weeping, brokenhearted, when she heard "the most peaceful, calming voice coming from one corner of the room. 'Don't worry,' it said, 'things will be better.'"

She saw no one, yet she could not deny the words she had heard. "I fell asleep almost immediately," she wrote, "and when I woke up I had a totally different outlook and was able to make my decision to divorce, move on. . . . But I will never forget that voice. I can still recall it today."

Sometimes the External Voice comes with music. Jody's mother was Jody's closest friend. As her mother was dying, Jody lay on the bed beside her, stroking her mother, telling her how beautiful she was and how much she loved her. Then her mother died. At first Jody was afraid to be in the house alone. Some two weeks after her mother's death, she was still sleeping on the living room couch, too afraid to enter her bedroom, where her mother had died. One night she was awakened by the most beautiful sound, she says, that she has ever heard. She could only describe it as angelic! It sounded like her mother's voice but younger. It wasn't singing a melody but rather a sequence of "la-la-la." She sat up. She even pinched herself to make sure she wasn't dreaming. The singing lasted for about three minutes, then stopped. She lay down and slept immediately. The next morning she felt such utter peace that all fears and grief had gone. She took the singing as a sign from her mother that she was all right, happy, in a better place.

"I wish I could hear it again," she wrote. "It was the most peaceful, calming, beautiful sound in the world—or rather not in this world."

I'm struck by how two different women, writing in different years and of two different experiences, used the same wording to describe "the most peaceful, calming, beautiful voice."

Judith Watkins Tartt is a paintings conservator. One evening her friend Michael said offhandedly, "If you haven't gone to Asia by the age of thirty-five, you haven't lived." The next morning she left her Connecticut Avenue studio to get a cup of coffee across the street. As she entered the coffee shop she saw a small Chinese man carrying a bag marked with the logo of the International Institute for Conservation, which had concluded its annual convention the day before. At her ear she heard a loud voice: *Speak to him!* She was so startled she turned to see who was behind her.

She obeyed. "Why are you still here?" was all she could think of to say. (She never spoke to strangers.)

"First time in America, I come to visit all conservation studios." He produced a list.

"Well, I'm a conservator," she said. "You can see my studio. It's just across the street." His name was Bobby Ng, and it turned out he was the chief conservator and museum developer of the Hong Kong Museum of Art. That evening after he had toured the National Gallery, the Freer, the Corcoran Gallery of Art and the Phillips, he arrived at her studio. She happened to have some pretty impressive paintings awaiting treatment, including a Fantin-Latour and a David Park.

They ate dinner that night at the nearby Chinese restaurant, and then she invited him to drive out to Virginia with her. "You can't leave America without seeing the countryside," she said. He wanted to go to a pistol-shooting range, where Judith, who had never held a gun in her hands, took aim and smashed the bull's-eye. He was thrilled. By the time he finished his dinner at the Red Fox Inn in Middleburg, he'd invited her to Hong Kong to do the conservation work on the fabulous collection of China Trade paintings at the Hong Kong Museum of Art.

And all because she'd heard a voice. Is that the same as intuition?

six

ANIMAL INTUITIVES

*I am sure of this, that by going much
alone a man will get more of a noble
courage in thought and word than from
all the wisdom that is in books.*

RALPH WALDO EMERSON,
Journal, 1833

I SUPPOSE MANY PEOPLE remember a happy childhood, but
mine seems an enchanted time to me now, cast in gold and silver
light in a time before TV and iPods and cell phones, e-mail and
text-messaging; before computers, Facebook, and Twitter; before
hi-fi surround-sound systems, Bluetooth, and hi-def—when we
roamed barefoot all summer, exploring our outdoor world. So important were animals that we children knew the names even of
our parents' and grandparents' long-dead favorite dogs. In the
course of a fairly long life I've known cats, horses, dogs, ducks,
cows, chickens, pigs; I've even kept honeybees, and as my daughters' mom I husbanded a host of pets, including gerbils, mice,
guinea pigs, goldfish, a box turtle, and one exceptional Dutch
rabbit.

On the other hand, it never occurred to me to "communicate" with them like Dr. Doolittle. Our animals indicated wants
or needs by ears, eyes, paws, tongues, hooves in an easily read-

able code. We also recognized that they knew much more about our inner lives.

There's no question that animals know everything we're thinking or, rather (and more important), what we are *feeling*: like children, they sense our inner states, absorb our emotions. Are we anxious, sad, fretful, confused? Are we angry, annoyed, vengeful, violent? Are we afraid? Are we pretending or preening with vanity and pride? The animals know it; they forgive us all.

Cats are especially intuitive. No wonder the Egyptians worshipped them as gods! (One man was pulled limb from limb by a mob after killing a cat.) For some five years now, Oscar, a black-and-white cat who has been visiting the Alzheimer's patients at the Steere House Nursing and Rehabilitation Center in Providence, Rhode Island, has been able to predict when a person is a few hours from death. He is never wrong. He never lingers unless the patient is at the point of death, and then he curls on the bed, purring, and does not leave until the patient succumbs. David Dosa, a geriatrician at the facility, did not believe it. He didn't even like cats, but he had to admit what he had seen. In 2007 he wrote an essay for the *New England Journal of Medicine* and later a book, *Making Rounds with Oscar.* How does the little cat know who will need his help to ease the journey to the other side?

I think the animals stand in as angels for us humans, teaching the qualities of mercy, tolerance, acceptance, trust. They have resilience and courage, and often a sense of humor, even playing little jokes. They love to play. They prick us out of our self-absorption and back to important things—like enjoying life. Animals that have been tortured and abused have other things to teach. Even with kindness, they may never fully recover, for, crippled by trauma and abuse, they become like frightened people, as it were, to draw forth our compassion and show us aspects of ourselves.

Our animals pull our emotions into themselves (how do they survive it?) and, by the purity of their own nature, transform our distress and pain. Merely resting in the presence of a good cat or dog or horse can call us into a sense of *Being*.

You groom a horse, and each brushstroke along those beautiful muscled withers and down its barrel soothes away troubles. Animals return us to the present moment. Your dog, gazing into your face, ready to take on any task you ask of him—or better yet to play—offers you solutions. The comfort you receive from a cat purring on your lap, its little paws kneading your stomach, or the sniffed kiss it tips daintily onto your lips—these are no small things. They heal a broken heart.

Once a cat I owned died a tragic, horrible death. I sat on the steps of my back porch looking out on my scruffy garden and wept, sobbing, the tears rolling down my chin. Then our pet rabbit hopped across the garden, jumped up into my lap, and lay across my knees. She sat there, comforting me, as my tears fell on her fur.

The psychic abilities of animals are renowned, and if telepathy and precognition were standards of intelligence, they'd be off the Richter scale, so that we humans would be relegated to serving them as their slaves. Animals predict earthquakes as well as seizures in their owners; they know when their owners are coming home; they travel incredible distances, in one recorded instance walking two thousand miles to find the way home; they pick up our intentions; they know when their owner has had an accident or died in a distant place. After his owner's death, one grieving dog found the burial site where he'd never been, and for weeks, with no footprints to follow and no aid from his sense of smell, he trotted eight miles to lie down on his master's grave. The story is reported in Rupert Sheldrake's excellent book *Dogs That Know When Their Owners Are Coming Home, and Other Unexplained Powers of Animals.*

I'm constantly amazed to read that some scientist has dug up a grant to discover whether animals think or feel—or whether they have a sense of humor! Have they never known an animal in their lives? Chimpanzees learn sign language; parrots and mynah birds repeat our words and know their meaning perfectly. The gentle bonobos demonstrate a social system so generous and tender that we crude humans might apprentice ourselves to learn their ways! If the animals are smart enough to know our thoughts, why can't we hear what they might have to say?

It turns out we can. Some people do.

Once when I was going through a particularly difficult time in my life, I drove out to the Great Falls of the Potomac with my beloved dog, Puck, a small corgi. There, I sat on a rock for a long time, simply staring at the tons of water that poured through the gorge, leaping and raging over rocks, and spraying white spume into the glittering blue air. I think I must have gazed at the same spot for twenty or thirty minutes, moving neither my body nor my eyes. I had no deep thoughts but merely gazed, distracted.

After a time I rose and began to climb over the rocks and craggy boulders to a higher vantage point, when suddenly behind me I heard a cry: "Wait! Wait for me!" I turned and saw my dog peering over the edge of a rock at me, his little legs too short to jump or clamber over. All I could see were his pointed ears, his pleading eyes. *Yet I had heard him speak. In English!* I went back and helped him over the boulder, amazed that I had not only picked up his distress but also heard him as an external voice.

In general I don't have the gift of hearing animals, unless finding my lost cat when she's trapped in the closet counts. I attribute my hearing Puck that day to my deep meditation as I watched the water tumbling over the falls.

My daughter's friend Ronda was caring for her mother's German shepherd at her house in Massachusetts when the dog disappeared. It was winter. Snow. She called and called. The dog was gone five days when she called an animal psychic, Brenda Cunliffe, who lived nearby. Brenda asked for the name of the dog and a description. Then she hooked up with the dog and after a moment began to speak.

"There's a big house with a white porch and columns. I'm on the porch, when a loud sound scares me [a car backfiring? a gunshot?]. I'm running down the road. I run into the woods and across a stream. I'm in the woods. I'm lost. I can't find my way back. I keep on for a long time. I come to a big, slippery meadow. It's hard to walk on. On the other side of the meadow is a little shack. I crawl under it. I'm hungry. I'm cold."

"I know exactly where he is!" cried Ronda. "He's at Fire Pond number five! Tell him I'm on my way."

And she went and picked him up.

The first time I ever heard of a pet psychic, or animal communicator as it is sometimes called, was in the early 1990s, when I was being interviewed at a Boston radio station. The radio host was saying goodbye to her earlier victim as I arrived, and as she welcomed me, she mentioned that the woman who had just left could talk to animals. *And so can I*, I thought, *but they don't answer back.*

"Did she talk to your dog?" I asked, pointing in amusement to the spaniel at her feet.

"That's exactly what I asked her halfway through the interview. She said, 'Oh, we've been talking all this time.' While we were on the air."

"Really. What did he say?" I was curious.

"She said he says he doesn't like to go down the basement stairs because they're too steep and he's afraid of falling. But he has to, because we feed him in the basement. And it's true!

"He said a new two-legged has come into the family, and he doesn't like her, and the cooking isn't as good as it was before."

"And?"

"Well, my mother has come to live with us, and she doesn't like the dog that much, and also she's taken over the cooking, since I work full-time."

I never found out the name of that animal communicator, but since that time the profession, it seems, has grown. Some find lost animals. Some specialize in expensive racehorses and show horses, and others offer help with your disturbed or psychotic house pets. If you hunt around, you can find classes in how to commune with animals.

A friend, Margaret Dulaney Balitsaris, lives on a farm in Pennsylvania. She loves her horse. He's learned to turn the barn lights on with his tongue, and she has to cover the light switch with duct tape when she puts him in his stall at night. The horse, injured, cannot be ridden, but Margaret walks beside him every day, talking to him and petting him. They're happy going for walks. She says she doesn't need to ride. They have a good time together.

One day, walking beside him, she watched his hind leg buckle under him. "I wonder what it feels like when your hind leg jerks and unhinges like that." The next step she took, she felt an electric current ripple down her leg. It made her leg collapse.

"Oh."

Was that animal communication?

The major problem with animals comes in verifying the information you receive. I'll explain what I mean. On Monday, April 27, 2009, Tinker Bell, a tiny, black, six-pound Chihuahua, was picked up in a freak tornado in Rochester Hills, Michigan, and carried away by seventy-mile-per-hour winds. Dorothy and Laverne Utley credit a pet psychic with guiding them to a wooded area nearly a mile away where they found the little puppy, tired, dirty, and hungry but alive. This kind of thing is easy to verify: You either find the dog, or you don't. (There's always the possibility that the animal walked off or was killed and eaten after the psychic found him, but if you find him you can pretty well trust that the animal intuitive knew what she was doing!)

I heard of one animal psychic who "gave a reading" to the half brother of the famous racehorse Secretariat. This horse was bold and sure of his own position in the world. He told her that he didn't like the little creature in the baby carriage that came sometimes to visit.

Speaking in Pictures

Animal communication is often done in pictures. Melody, a cowgirl who lives in Taos, New Mexico, had a horse with whom she communicated through images. She could never catch him in the pasture if she was upset or rushing (no one could), but if she sent pictures of stroking and petting him lovingly and of what fun they had riding in the high meadows, of galloping through the tall grass, of drinking from streams that gurgled over brown rocks, the horse would lift his head and walk to her, bending for the halter. She had to feed him love-feast pictures. When she was forced to sell him, she says he turned and gave her such an aggrieved look as she has never forgotten.

Sometimes, however, the information comes in scrambled form.

A few years ago, my daughter Sarah found that one of her two cats was so jealous of her baby that she had to give him away—the cat, I mean. Ishi, a magnificent black cat who was part Siamese, to judge by the shape of his face, was young, wild, and energetic. After he scratched the baby, however, my daughter informed me (in the direct way children use with a mother) that when I came to visit the following week, Ishi would be going back to Washington with me; she thought a cousin in Virginia might give him a permanent home.

I wasn't happy, but I flew to Massachusetts and arranged to bring Ishi back to stay with me until he could move on to his new home. Meanwhile, to ease his likely distress, we asked a pet psychic to explain the change to Ishi, but as you'll see, it's sometimes easier to know what the cat is thinking than to have him imagine an incomprehensible event. On the day of his departure, petting and soothing him, we gave him a tranquilizer and drove him, asleep in his little crate, to the plane.

Arrived at my apartment in Washington, I slid the still-dopey cat into the kitchen and shut the door, confining him to a small, safe space where he had food and water and soft bedding for the night.

The next day I faced a panther! Terrified, he hissed and slashed at me with his claws. Moreover, it turned out that the cousin couldn't take Ishi as planned; the cat was mine. For a week he challenged me, ears back, teeth bared. He hated me.

Finally, I called another animal intuitive. She talked to Ishi long-distance and relayed his story to me over the phone. When he was young (she said) and vulnerable, he'd lived with two girls who'd tried to poison him. They gave him drugs for fun. One of them wanted to kill him. Now, on his own, he didn't know where he was, and he was frightened.

I was astonished. Was she making this up? Ishi had never

lived with two young college girls, much less drug addicts! Sarah had adopted both Ishi and his mother from the pound when he was only a few weeks old, and he had never lived with anyone else, much less someone who'd tried to kill him!

Disappointed, I paid the pet psychic and dismissed her entire story. A week later, Ishi and I had a breakthrough, and in the months that followed we became so deeply bonded that later still, when I was forced to give him away (allergies), I wept. He was a beautiful creature, sweet, loving, attentive, gentle. I found a wonderful home for him. I know he's happy there.

It was only long afterward that it dawned on me what the animal intuitive had meant: She'd seen the situation in images from Ishi's point of view; the "two young girls" were my daughter and myself! We *had* tranquilized him for the plane, and when he'd woken up, he was in a strange place without his family or owner. He thought I'd meant to kill him. And so I learned that while you can hear what the animal has to say, you might have a hard time interpreting it. They are not thinking in words, after all, but in images—in "knowings"—in the same way they pick up telepathically our thoughts and emotions.

WHAT DOES IT FEEL LIKE to "communicate" with an animal? Once, many years ago, I met an Australian fisherman who talked to dolphins. Whenever he went out fishing, he found that dolphins swarmed around his boat and, moreover, that he could ask them to jump and they would jump or to follow and they would accompany his boat, diving and cavorting around and under and ahead of him. He called to them by mental telepathy.

We were at an environmental conference held at the Freer Gallery of Art when he told me this. I was intrigued.

"I can do it to you, if you want," he offered.

"Do what?"

"Make you come to me."

"You're not serious!"

Who could resist such an offer? I walked outside and down the gracious sandstone stairway of the art gallery to the pavement below, and there I stood a moment wondering how he would "call" me to him and how I would recognize it if he did. It was a lovely soft dusky summer evening. Indoors, in the reception hall, a crowd of environmentalists was shouting happily at one another, creating an awful din as they battled for drinks and hors d'oeuvres. I took a breath, looking across the grassy sweep of the Washington Mall.

Suddenly, and I can't explain why exactly, I felt a "need," a longing, a desire to take a few steps toward the gallery. As I moved toward the stairs, it felt "right," and so I mounted the stairwell, still not quite certain what I was doing but following the instinct, the intuition, as if pulled by a beam of light. I imagine an airplane on automatic pilot, when hooked onto the landing beam at the airport, as it descends with this same surety and sense of *yes*. I pushed open the Freer Gallery doors, turned left, and moved confidently down the stairs to the lower gallery, and there before me the whole great mass of this gathering spread out, and suddenly I woke up. Lost. The "pull" had stopped. Where was I supposed to go?

I found my Australian talking to a couple. He turned in apology. "I'm so sorry!" he said. "I was interrupted. How far did you get?"

I told him I'd made it to the entrance.

"And then a gentleman came up to talk to me," he said. "I couldn't do it anymore. But you got most of the way." He was pleased with his success.

I never found out exactly how he "called" me to him or what

he did to bring the dolphins to his side. It's a gift you'd think would be useful. Particularly if you have children who tend to wander off.

DOLPHINS ARE ESPECIALLY TELEPATHIC. Once, sitting on a dock in Florida near a bottlenose dolphin pool, I "sent" the thought request for a dolphin to leap out of the water for me! I wanted to see him jump. No, that's wrong. It was all about my ego. I wanted to see if he would pick up my telepathy and do what I asked. Could he hear me? I "beamed" and "beamed" at him. In vain. He swam on in his slow, bored circles.

Oh.

Finally I gave up. I pushed to my feet, started to move away, and just then saw him swimming in ever-faster circles round and round his pond, gaining speed—and he jumped! And jumped! And jumped again in front of me.

They get our messages.

The trick is, can we hear the ones they send to us?

MARIA KARMI is an animal intuitive in Finland. When she wants to communicate with an animal on behalf of the owner, or with her own animals, or with wild ones, she puts herself into a mode of deep listening. If she tries to guess what the problem is, she will fail, she says, but if she grows quiet and receptive, if she moves into the silence, the information comes. She does not push or strive for anything.

"That's why communication is so easy. I just need to listen. The animal tells me what it wants me to know. All I need to do is trust the information that is given me."

As a child, Maria spent hours alone on her grandparents' farm. She was very sensitive to emotions and could "read" people around her, as well as the animals. In the silence of nature she felt a part of something larger. Later, when she was fifteen, her curiosity took her to out-of-body experiences so frightening that she promised herself and God in heaven that she would always stay connected to her own body and to the earth. Now she works as a physiotherapist, dedicated to mindfulness, Chinese medicine, and the practice of Being Here Now. Her body, she says, is her anchor, and to do any telepathic work with animals she must stay grounded and physically strong.

Six years ago she took a class in animal communication. She asked her dog Ruffe, a nine-year-old border collie, "Is there anything I can do for you?" He placed his paw on her knee and answered in clear Swedish (her native tongue): "Just try to love me. That's all I need." She was so overwhelmed that she wept for an hour. Her grey parrot Chino told her that he was afraid of the dark, after which she took care to leave a night-light on when it was time to sleep. Her rabbit XI said he was afraid of heights, and indeed she could feel how his little stomach twisted when she picked him up.

Later she took a course in communicating with problem horses and gained confidence by checking her intuitions with the owners. She was amazed how easy it was! "Since then," she wrote to me, "I have had many amazing chats with animals of different species, and every one of them is different. It makes me very humble when they open up to me. I'm so grateful to be able to give them voice. We have so much to learn from the animals; they touch the human heart in ways that no therapy in the world can do.

"We meet at a soul level," she continued. "If I close my eyes when communicating, I couldn't tell you if I were listening to a human or an animal. The feelings are universal."

I HAVE ONE LAST STORY concerning animals. I have a place in New Mexico. One summer while I was out there, I started horseback riding again. I was raised with horses but had stopped years before. Suddenly I felt an urge to ride. I was put on a half-Arabian three-year-old named Spring. She was amazing! I adored her. I know horses, and I felt somehow that she was special. The following summer I leased her for several months. We had such a deep connection that the stable owner urged me to buy her, but I refused. How could I keep a horse when I traveled so much, dividing my time between Washington and New Mexico? The horse would always be wherever I wasn't. Still, I loved this animal, and I knew that she loved me.

A young woman named Danielle bought her. I arranged to lease her whenever I came to New Mexico—a happy compromise for me: I got to ride this lovely horse without the responsibility of owning her.

One morning in December 2007 I woke out of a deep sleep with the horrified premonition: "Spring is going to be sold, and this time she'll move far away; I won't ever see her again."

I e-mailed the New Mexico stable. "If Spring is ever sold, will you let me know?"

The answer shot back: "I just learned that her owner has to leave Taos. She told me she wants to sell the horse."

I put down an option to buy her and arranged to spend a month in New Mexico. I said I'd decide by the end of the month whether to buy the horse or not. And then came weeks of indecision! It made no sense whatsoever for me to buy a horse. It's expensive. I travel. I've never wanted to own a horse. It's easy to buy a horse and hard to sell one. Was she a good horse, anyway? I didn't know. Just because I'd fallen in love with *her*, did that mean anything? She had a strange conformation, but an exquisite head and a sweetness of nature I'd never met before in a horse. When she saw me coming, she'd walk the length of the paddock to meet me. I loved to ride her. I loved her willingness, her lightness, her intelligence, her efforts to do whatever I asked.

But buying a horse made no sense!

I didn't *want* a horse! Why did I feel I was "supposed" to buy her? That we were "supposed" to be together?

Believe me, this time I consulted not one psychic but two. One said there was a karmic connection between the two of us and, yes, buy her. The other said I should not. I believed the second.

Each time I made the decision to let Spring go, congratulating myself and experiencing a welcome sense of relief, I was struck an hour later by the nagging sense that the decision had to be revisited.

But buying a horse was nuts! I didn't even know where I would keep her!

How could I afford a horse?

It would change my whole life!

And so I passed that month, waffling back and forth, until one day it occurred to me that every time I have followed an intuition *that made no sense*, it's always worked out right and that I don't have the prescience to foresee an outcome. That I must trust. Trust God. Trust these unexplained psychic powers. Trust my inner wisdom, the angels that bring me gifts or lessons that I don't even know I want. Trust that if the Universe is giving me the horse, then it will also somehow provide the money to stable her, or if it doesn't the horse could be sold. Or given away. Trust. I had to trust my guides, my God, the Beloved that bends, brooding, over us, offering us new ways.

I bought Spring. I have brought her to Virginia, where I ride, and she has given me more pleasure than I would have imagined possible. I don't understand our connection; I don't need to. One day, while I was grooming her magnificent hindquarters (and growing quiet under the spell of her sweet scent), she swung her tail around as if to switch a fly, draped it over my face and shoulders, and held it there, veiling me in her embrace.

Inviting Intuition II: Deep Listening

There are tried, true ways to develop intuition, but only the brave person is willing to undertake the path.

First, you go into stillness. Practice being alone and in silence.

Take a walk. Look around. Sit on a park bench. Be still.

In rest you experience heightened awareness, discernment, empathy, joy.

Close your eyes and listen to the wind. If it is possible to get out into the country, out into nature . . . go!

Second, practice mindfulness and meditation. It doesn't matter what form of meditation you are drawn to as long as you begin. (I give instructions in the appendix for anyone who wants them.) Sit for five or ten or twenty minutes once or twice a day. Close your eyes. Allow your thoughts to drift. Go inward, and watch your breathing ("In . . . out . . ."). Watch with *attention*. Gradually your stormy thoughts calm down. You grow still. Now you can sense the nudge of intuition, listen for "the still, small voice of God." Do this every day. It is mind-training. It changes your brain waves. It's not for nothing that some forms of meditation are called Insight Meditation.

Meditation alters the brain. It makes you *happy*!

One study of high school students found that those who meditated *for only five or ten minutes twice a day* showed prefrontal structural changes. The prefrontal part of the brain governs discernment, wisdom, and moral judgment. It's the CEO of the brain. Computerized brain imaging has shown great cavities and gouges in the prefrontal brains of a good proportion of the youngsters being studied. Yet by meditating for only five minutes in the morning and again in the evening—and this was with no chanting of mantras, no religious practices, but simply sitting quietly, watching the breath *for only two weeks*—those gorges and caverns filled in.

Third, trust the messages you start to receive. Insight is different from the shivers of anxiety, worry, or fear, and it differs from conscious thought.

Keep a journal of intuitions or spiritual encounters. How does intuition present itself to you? You'll soon come to trust your Inner Director, your guardian angels, your Higher Self.

Talk to it. Ask for help.

Then listen.

To increase intuition, avoid drugs, alcohol, and mind-altering substances. The clean brain is automatically intuitive.

BEING STILL

It takes courage to be quiet. I know people for whom this is easy. They are by nature introverts. They are often artists or scientists, exceptionally creative. They hike off to a hermitage without neighbors nearby. Or they go fishing on a beautiful river, camping alone, waking with the golden streaks of dawn and watching the light that sparkles off the water. They catch their breath at the beauty of a field of grass moving like ocean waves in the wind. They lie down in green pastures, they restore their soul in solitude.

I know other people to whom being alone is so painful they would rather hurl themselves at a ball on a squash court, bench-press massive weights, take math tests, lose chess games, toss pancakes in a fast-food diner—anything—rather than be imprisoned with their own thoughts.

"Why ever would I want to look inside? What if there's nothing there?" cried one woman I know. Which would be funny except that she was serious. And another acquaintance, stiff with righteous resolve: "Meditation is so self-centered. I think you should be out doing things for someone else if you have so much time on your hands."

It takes discipline to be still. Yet what you discover is a boundless expansion of awareness. Pure consciousness. Also, your brain works better. Studies indicate that meditation—being still—merely *being* eases stress, eases addictions, builds up the immune system, and provides physical and emotional well-being.

It also increases intuition. You know who is calling on the phone. You lose your car keys, search everywhere, then remember to pause and send out a silent plea to the Beloved, the Holy Spirit, your guides and guardians: "Help!" If you are open, then, you find yourself walking to a table and pulling the keys out from under a pile of papers. Intuition?

And one other thing about meditation: As you strengthen spiritually, as you increase your vibratory frequency, you shine with light. It's called *enlightenment*.

Listen. I have seen light pouring off people and off grasses and trees, and animals, and children—off every living thing. It flames off us "like shining from shook foil," as the poet Gerard Manley Hopkins wrote, for we ourselves are composed of Divine fire, and this is why we can see spirits and guides when our spiritual eyes are opened. We are stardust. We are composed of the same structures and substance that blew out of the Big Bang, born of the "suchness" of God, the entangled photons that confuse and tease our physicists.

We are Divine.

Not long ago I saw a woman, praying. A shock of light passed over her, streaming from her skin. Light poured from her third eye, the spiritual center.

I have been witness many times to this phenomenon, although it is usually glimpsed in a veiled or shadowy way, a passing, fleeting quickening of light that flares up in a person and dies down again.

It is the light of love.

seven

VARIATIONS ON A THEME

*What we achieve inwardly will change
outer reality.*

PLUTARCH

AT THIS POINT it's appropriate to confess that for some years
I've worked as an intuitive or psychic and sometimes as a medium; so it behooves us to pause a moment for some definitions.
Because the difference between intuition and psychic abilities
is one only of degree, like the difference between the child
plunking out "Twinkle, Twinkle, Little Star" on the piano and
well-practiced fingers rippling over a Chopin étude. It's a matter
of *practice*, but they're both playing notes!

How many people in our country consult the tarot, or throw
the I Ching, or visit an astrologer, or read the runes? How many
go to a palmist, intuitive, psychic, or medium to learn what Fate
may hold? Lots more than we imagine, and lots more in times
of recession than in financial booms, according to a November 23, 2008, article in *The New York Times*. Moreover, these
clients are often wealthy professionals, like an executive from
Seagate Technology, the $11-billion-a-year maker of hard drives
for PlayStation 3, or from William Morris, the talent agency; or
a Manhattan attorney; or a Hollywood producer, all consulting

the same intuitive, Laura Day, to whom they pay $10,000 a month for help with their financial decisions.

I WAS HAVING DINNER one summer at a lovely restaurant in Bar Harbor, Maine, with three other women. It was a sweet summer evening. We watched the boats rock on the water lapping at the green slope of the lawn. The sun was going down, the golden light softening to grey dusk. Clair, a pediatrician, works in genetics in Baltimore, and Judy is a professor emeritus of pediatrics and medical genetics at a children's hospital in British Columbia. The third in our party, Barbara, is a science writer. I listened in awe as their conversation swung from genes and genomes to childhood diseases or to famous scientists they knew at this convention, including their Nobel-laureate friends. At one point Judy turned to me. She has a gentle way of tilting her head toward you, eyes soft, smiling with encouragement. She should be painted by a Renaissance genius.

"But I'm interested in what you're doing," she said. "Intuition and the paranormal. Tell me."

One 2003 study showed 50 percent of women are *not* telepathic, but 85 percent of telepathics are female. The typical intuitive is young, educated, creative, often left-handed or ambidextrous, and able to concentrate and focus.

An animated discussion about whether intuition and psychic experiences are unusual ensued. Judy murmured that she was intuitive, but she felt her medical diagnoses were based on experience, nothing else. Clair, on the other hand, felt she had had psychic experiences, but she wasn't sure that everyone had this gift. They both agreed that if an infant doesn't develop a sensory organ by the age of two, the innate ability is lost. A blindfolded child, for example, will be unable to see. The great proportion of Asian children, who are exposed to tonal languages in which meaning is expressed by pitch, develop perfect pitch, whereas only a small percentage of Western children have perfect pitch. Is it the same with psychic abilities? Would that explain why some people have the talent and others don't?

I argued that it's just a skill that can be learned. The brain is a fluid instrument, and I told them of Joseph Fuchs, the famous violinist, who in his seventies lost the use of the fingers in his left hand—his fingering hand. He taught himself to play again, and in his nineties was still giving solo concerts in Carnegie Hall. The brain finds pathways. It grows throughout your life. Why would it be different for psychic abilities?

"How do you do it?" Clair asked, twirling her wineglass. "What do you do?"

Surprised, I set down my fork. No one had asked me this before, and I felt shy. But they were serious. Curious. Suddenly the words came pouring out, incautiously, the story I'd not ever told before. And because of that, I can tell it later in this book. Not here. But further on. And not because my way is special or better than that of hosts of intuitives and sensitives but because it's my experience; at least I can tell how it feels for me.

THE WORD PSYCHIC COMES from the Greek word meaning "soul," which searches endlessly for Love. It is said that we all knew love once, in that other place, before we were born, and that we will experience it again at death, while our lifetime here is spent in yearning for that lost, half-remembered state when we recognized our very soul, our psyche.

In the beautiful Greek myth, the young girl Psyche (the soul) is deeply in love with her husband, Eros, god of Love, and he with her. Each night he comes to her bed; each dawn he leaves before she sees his face. Psyche is filled with happiness. Her jealous sisters whisper in her ear. "How can you love him?" they ask. "You don't even know what he looks like. Perhaps he's a monster. How do you know? Take a candle," they enjoin her, "and when he's asleep, light it. Look on him."

Lighting her candle, she holds it up and gasps. He is so beautiful! But a drop of melting wax falls on his skin. He wakes up. He tells Psyche that now he must go away, according to the law set down by his mother, Aphrodite. Psyche will not be able to find him until she walks through nine pairs of iron shoes and nine iron staves, searching for him everywhere. He leaves. Then bravely she sets out after him, searching for her husband, Love. In the story Psyche finds Eros, and they are joined once again, and we're told that this is the spiritual journey that each soul takes to find her Self, which is the same as finding love.

Defining Terms

If you have heightened or extrasensory perception (ESP), if you experience the paranormal, including telepathy and healing touch, animal communication, clairvoyance, and precognition, you are said to be *psychic*. The word is used both as a noun and an adjective. You may be psychic or have had a psychic experience.

On the other hand, if you are giving a psychic or intuitive reading, and a spirit appears at your elbow, you are acting as a medium, mediating between the visible and invisible worlds. Many say that it is the chemistry of the medium, the frequency of her electromagnetic vibration, that allows the spirit to form the wispy, white ectoplasm that we see. From the time of the Delphic Oracle, such visions have been revered.

The Dalai Lama notes in one of his books of the need to understand "the whole phenomenon of emanation." The degree of autonomy of a vision or emanation, he says, "depends upon the level of realization of the individual who is creating the emanation, that is, the emanator. At a lower level," he notes, "an emanation created by an individual is to a certain extent monitored and controlled by the emanator, almost as if by computer. On the other hand, in the case of an individual who has very high spiritual realizations, then the emanated beings may be fairly autonomous."

He adds that he wishes he'd had such mystical experiences himself. "But no luck! There are quite a few questions I would like to ask!"

We'll talk later about seeing spirits and acting as an intuitive or medium. It requires a certain spiritual purification and a discipline that most people are unwilling to undertake. What does it mean to be "spiritual"? I'm not sure, actually. But the fruits are easy to recognize. They are: forgiveness, tolerance, generosity, and patience. I would add humility, tenderness, wisdom, and understanding—the very attributes we'd like extended to ourselves. Where and how are these qualities found? In the Great Silence. In those moments when, communing with the psyche, we hear the still, small Voice of God.

Part II

THE AWAKENED MIND

The Tibetan Buddhist model for the awakened mind is orgasm, because it is only at the climax of lovemaking that the evils of ignorance drop away.

WILLIAM BUCK

eight

LIGHT OF YOUR LIFE

We aren't physical beings having a
spiritual experience. We're spiritual
beings having a physical experience.

ANONYMOUS

EMANUEL SWEDENBORG, son of a bishop, lived from 1688 to 1772. Brilliant, creative, intellectual, he was a scientist, inventor, philosopher, theologian, and linguist, and he had an enormous influence on the great minds of the next centuries, from Blake and Goethe to Elizabeth Barrett Browning, Emerson, Balzac, Yeats, Borges, Strindberg, Carl Jung, and Helen Keller. He was also clairvoyant. One evening at a dinner party in London he shot to his feet with horror, exclaiming that a great fire had broken out in Stockholm, 286 miles away, that it had already consumed his neighbor's house and now threatened his own. He paced the room, watching the far-off event. Two hours later, he dropped into a chair, reporting with relief that the fire had stopped three doors from his house. It took two days to confirm the news, down to the precise hour that he had seen the fire.

In 1745, at the age of sixty-seven, Swedenborg had a mystical revelation (a series of them, actually), and for the last twenty-seven years of his life he communed with spirits and angels, writing volumes of his experiences that exploded the entire theology of his demon-ridden superstitious age, with his expositions of a deity of mercy and loving kindness, a God available and accessible to every individual through spiritual intuition and without the mediation of priests. It is in these writings, often obscure and obfuscated, that he described the human journey as the transformation from a materialistic to a spiritual awareness, when with our spiritual insight we see into far-off realms.

IT WAS CHRISTMAS. I waited at a hospital in Washington, D.C., to see my doctor. It was crowded and the doctor was running late. I scowled. I checked my watch. I jiggled my foot. I had things to do, presents to buy, bills to pay, people to call, Christmas to get through, and here I was (checking my watch) *kept waiting!* The tinsel decorations annoyed me. The nurses and clerks, harried and overworked, fueled my aggravation. The more impatient and irritable I became, the worse I felt, until in a flash of understanding it occurred to me that my impatience (or, rather, the *feeding* and *nursing* of my annoyance) was only making me feel worse. But how to calm the frenzied, frantic clatter of my mind?

"God, help me," I prayed. "Show me—"

I blinked. Everyone around me—the clerks behind the desk, the nurses with their clipboards, the woman struggling down the hall on crutches—was bathed in light. I was so startled I sat up. It was like seeing the heat waves shimmering above a hot tar road in summer: everyone rippling with light. The clerks were not merely physical bodies typing and filing behind their desks but beings of Light, and what was strange was that no one knew that they were shining, luminous. Each one was absorbed by personal concerns or deadlines or pain or emotional turmoil, when in fact (was I mad?) they were spiritual beings, moving lights. In that moment even the tinsel took on deeper meaning, no longer the pitiful symbol of enforced merriment but a sweet and poignant reminder of hope in a season that for many people offers only bleak loneliness and despair: the tinsel of gratitude, the silver shining fish of faith.

For the next week every living thing I saw, every tree or bush or dog, every person, every living sentient thing was surrounded by and *emanating* light. Was this what the Bible meant when it said that we are made in the image of God? I was filled with a melting gratitude, with profound forgiveness and relief, for if all these others were Light Beings, haloed with golden light, then *so was I!*

> *. . . thou, celestial light,*
> *Shine inward, and the mind through all her powers*
> *Irradiate; there plant eyes, all mist from thence*
> *Purge and disperse, that I may see and tell*
> *Of things invisible to mortal sight.*
>
> JOHN MILTON

FOR MILLENNIA people have seen auras around certain living things. In the Middle Ages, artists depicted all the spiritual giants—Christ, the Madonna, apostles, angels, saints—with a golden nimbus at their heads. And not only in medieval Europe was this radiance perceived, but in Buddhist cultures, Hindu paintings: a corona of light pouring from angels and gods.

There is a story that one night Saint Francis and Saint Clare met in conversation, and the light from their love, inflamed by their talk of God, was so great that it lit up the Umbrian hillside around them. Is it metaphor?

For centuries in the high Himalayas of Tibet, where the

temperatures drop to thirty below zero as howling winds lash the mountaintops with snow, certain monks have engaged in the age-old practice of *g'tumo* to stoke the fire of their inner energy. They sit in meditation in the freezing cold, and the heat and light they produce are so intense that the snow melts in a little circle around them. In this practice they eat little. They may not build a fire to warm themselves, for a physical fire would prevent them from achieving the inner heat of *g'tumo*.

It takes years to reach this goal.

I'm not suggesting that we can all acquire such abilities—or that we should even want to. But without our doing anything at all, we emit an aura or energy field. And didn't Christ tell us this? Didn't he admonish us not to "hide your light under a bushel-basket?" Another time, speaking in the positive voice (Matthew 5:16), didn't He direct us to "Let your light so shine before men, that they may see your good works and glorify your Father in heaven"?

Scientists know a great deal now about the electromagnetic and subtle energies emitted by all living things that until recently have eluded measurement. Today any number of research institutions are mapping and studying subtle energies. Books on the subject now appear regularly, and most people speak easily these days of chakras—those wheels of whirling energy in the human body that emit light and reflect our state of health (animals have chakras, too, but we don't talk so much of these). We acknowledge the ancient Chinese acupuncture meridians, along which our natural energies stream. Changes in energy can be measured by the ion flow, and there is, in fact, a dedicated organization, the International Society for the Study of Subtle Energies and Energy Medicine (ISSEEM), which held its twentieth American conference in Colorado in the summer of 2010. Dr. Andrew Weil, in Tucson, is teaching subtle energies to students in medical school. Edgar Mitchell, the former astronaut, founded the Institute of Noetic Studies (IONS) specifically to study paranormal and subtle energies; and ordinary people all over the world practice shifting and enlarging their *chi* with tai chi or qi gong and other martial arts. They pay healers and energy practitioners to work on their multimillion-dollar show dogs. Moreover, a number of devices now measure the subtle auras that previously were visible only to psychics and mystics.

As a man who has devoted his whole life to the most clear-headed science, to the study of matter, I can tell you as the result of my research about atoms this much: There is no matter as such! All matter originates and exists only by virtue of a force which brings the particles of an atom to vibration and holds this most minute solar system of the atom together . . . We must assume behind this force the existence of a conscious and intelligent Mind. This Mind is the matrix of all matter.

MAX PLANCK

THE FIRST PERSON TO CLAIM he photographed the aura was Russian electrician Semyon Kirlian, who in 1939 accidentally discovered that if an object is placed directly on a metal photographic plate and charged with a high voltage, small discharges (created by the electric field at the edges of the object) create the image of a corona on the photographic plate. Kirlian's work, from 1939 onward, was variously called electrography, electrophotography, and corona discharge photography.

I remember being fascinated in the 1970s by these photos. People were photographing leaves, shrimp, their own hands, the ears of dogs, and we marveled at the extraordinary bands of light shooting off the leaf, the shrimp, our fingertips. Experimenters cut a leaf in two and recorded the way the light at the mutilation shrank back, as if in pain. They called it the phantom limb effect. Even more astonishing were the effects of radical cruelty on nearby living things. Perhaps you have seen some of these photographs, in which the light field of a healthy plant seems to recoil at the murder of a shrimp across the room. Do even lower life forms, like plants or shrimp, we wondered, have consciousness?

Look on the Internet, and you'll find some 115 million sites for auras, some 2.36 million for Kirlian, and another 5,300 or so for the incorrect spelling of "Kirlean," so that you could spend your life clicking on these and never have time for any other activity, including reading the book in your hand. A goodly number deny the veracity of auras. The Kirlian image depends on film voltage, they explain, on perspiration, pressure of the fingertip or other object on the metal, on humidity, the exposure time, and various other variables.

Even *inanimate* objects, it turns out, reveal a nimbus of light. A coin pressed hard upon the plate and an artificial plastic flower display the same "bioelectric energy aura" as a living leaf . . . provided the coin or plastic flower is moist. It is the moisture, the water, that creates the effect.

Today the detractors of Kirlian photography are as passionate as atheists and often just as witty. One of these is Rory Coker, professor of physics at the University of Texas, Austin, who has devoted a website to ASTOP, the Austin Society to Oppose Pseudoscience.

"Kirlian himself had no idea of [what he was doing]," he writes in scathing denunciation. "Pictures of streamers have been taken for more than 100 years (engineers usually call them Nasser photographs) and the streamer phenomenon is perfectly understood."

Heaping scorn on Kirlian photography, he reports, that "a human body (and every other object in the universe that is not at absolute zero temperature) emits electro-magnetic radiation. A human being emits about the same power (100 Watts) in infrared radiation that a standard light bulb does in visible radiation. This has nothing whatsoever to do," he concludes, "with 'Kirlian' photography."

I recommend his site for its sheer entertainment. It takes on chakras, auras, nineteenth-century spiritual ectoplasm, and kundalini yoga.

Fortunately, the story of photographing human energy does not end there. There is also "aura photography," in which a colorful image of a person's face and upper body is produced by interpreting galvanic skin responses and adding color to the photograph with a printer. In aura photography, no high voltage is involved, as with Kirlian photos, and neither does the object come into direct contact with the film. But it, too, has its detractors.

Meanwhile, current research continues with still a third method, the gas discharge visualization device (GDV), developed by Dr. Konstantin G. Korotkov at what is now the Saint Petersburg (Russia) National Research University of Information Technologies, Mechanics and Optics. This device measures electrophotonic glow by use of glass electrodes that create a pulsed electrical field excitation, called perturbation technique. The GVD has been certified by the Russian ministry of health for use in hospitals and athletic training programs as a general clinical diagnostic tool to detect stress. I know one respected pediatrician who uses it with her little patients.

The device has been studied by the National Institutes of Health, and I'm told that the State of Israel tested the physical and emotional health of their military pilots with GVDs before allowing them to fly a mission and that it has inspired interest as an antiterrorist screening device at airports. (Apparently if the device shows a skewed energy field, indicating undue stress, the harried passenger is pulled aside for questioning.)

I FIRST CAME ACROSS the GDV device some years ago in Taos, New Mexico, when Krishna Madappa gave me a demonstration. Krishna is a lean, slender, handsome man with a bouncing energetic step. By his own admission he is a holistic healer, teacher, storyteller, shaman, and distiller of essential oils. He is also interested in the scientific explanation of energy fields. He is an extravagant and charismatic man with a brilliant smile and ebullient, infectious enthusiasm.

When he offered to test the device on me, I accepted instantly. The instrument appears quite simple. Inserting your arm through a long black sleeve that shields all external light, you place your fingertips on a glass plate that transfers a computerized image onto a screen.

Always curious, I thrust my arm happily through the black cloth sleeve and pressed my fingertips to the glass plate, straining to see the image on his laptop. On the screen I could see the computerized outline of a human body surrounded by four bands of color. The thick outer blue stripe represented physical health. Next to this and closer to the line drawing of the body was a thin layer of violet, representing the subject's emotional state at the time of the reading (jealousy, anxiety, grief, anger, sorrow, curiosity, happiness, serenity, etc.). The next-closest layer showed jagged pink lines denoting the psychological state (reactions to past traumas, present states of mind). And finally, stretched tight against the computer-imaged outline of the body was a yellowish-orange slip of color that Krishna said depicted the spiritual field, the relationship of inner to outer.

Looking at my aura as outlined on the monitor, I saw that all four colors streamed out with healthy vital force everywhere *except* at my right knee, where all four colors collapsed into a black hole. I was shocked. This marked the exact spot where I'd had surgery after a ski injury some years earlier.

Krishna was delighted. If I would try an experiment, he said, he'd show me how quickly my energy field could heal. Of course I agreed. He had me drink two quarts of a delicious, super-hydrating, structured, "oxygenated" water, named Angel Fire Water, that comes from the nearby town of Angel Fire. Even in the dry climate of New Mexico, it's hard to down two quarts of water in a few minutes, but I managed to glug down both bottles and to slosh back to the photographic equipment, feeling my stomach uncomfortably distended. When he took a reading of my finger-tips this second time, all four colors flared forth on his laptop more powerfully than before and with no injury visible at the knee.

Such are the conductive and healing properties of water.

> *I shall not commit the fashionable stupidity of regarding everything I cannot explain as a fraud.*
>
> C. G. JUNG

A FEW MONTHS EARLIER, in Sedona, Arizona, Krishna Madappa had taken "readings" of the well-known trance medium Summer Bacon, recording her energy at the beginning of, during, and after the trance state. (Not all psychics go into deep trance, but Summer Bacon is one who does, and then she becomes a channel for the white-bearded Scottish spiritual giant and nineteenth-century visionary Reverend James Martin Peebles [1822–1922], an author, healer, lecturer, and former consul to Trebizond in Turkey. Peebles is busy serving another medium, too, the Reverend F. Reed Brown, former pastor of the Arlington Metaphysical Chapel in Virginia, who, like Bacon, channels this master.) When in trance, Bacon's voice changes to that of Peebles. Her words are informed with the higher consciousness of the spirit who permeates her field. Madappa had saved the session on his laptop, and as he showed it to me now, I could clearly see the strong, golden light that surrounded her in both the trance state and immediately afterward, before she gradually faded back to her normal resting state. After her trance, she craves water and sometimes a shot of alcohol, Madappa reported, to restore herself. She needs to go off alone and be quiet until her natural energy flow returns.

I'M NOT GOING TO GET into the dispute about whether these machines are recording the true aura or not. The fact is, anyone can learn to see the aura. (Why not, if we emit the 100 watts of a standard lightbulb?) We call it the vital life force. It's what the leading French philosopher and Nobel laureate Henri Bergson named the *élan vitale*. (Bergson, who died in 1941, wrote of "mind-energy" and was convinced that immediate experience and intuition were more important than rationalism for an understanding of reality.)

Once I was in a tai chi class given by a renowned master. At the end of the daylong session, I went up to him and asked him, laughing, if he could throw out a ray of invisible energy and knock someone down, the way I'd seen it done in the movies. He nodded gravely. He could. I asked (ever cheeky) if he would demonstrate on me. He answered no, he wouldn't want to hurt me, but he would demonstrate the power on his three male apprentices.

We students all stood back. He held his right arm out at roughly shoulder height, his wrist flexed carelessly. The three strong, burly youths glanced at each other, wiped their hands on their pants, lined up, and *threw* themselves at his hand. Of course, three men can't all push at the same time on one small square, but while one of them thrust with all his strength on the master's palm and wrist, his feet scrabbling for purchase on the artificial turf, the other two backed him up, adding their weight and strength against the master. We could see their teeth clenched, their feet paddling the floor in their efforts to rock their teacher from his steady stance. Their faces were taut and strained. He stood unmoved, gazing vaguely into the distance.

Suddenly all three boys flew backward, arms pinwheeling, scrambling for balance, all arms, knees, elbows, legs. One hit the far wall before he fell to the floor.

It was a persuasive demonstration of what we beginning students were trying to learn as we caught our feeble balls of energy and shifted them in slow tai chi movements around ourselves.

MANY TIMES AFTER I'VE GIVEN a workshop or talk on angels, or mysticism, or prayer, or love, I've had women come up to me (why do women seem to sense these more than men?) to tell me they've seen the most beautiful colors—gold, pinks, blues— flaring around me as I spoke. I used to look at them bemused. Were they nuts? I myself do not see colored auras. I nodded courteously, and thanked them, but in those days I discounted their words, knowing how dramatic (and flaky) some people are. I thought it would be sort of nice to see an aura, which I imagined like the aurora borealis flaming out: a rainbow of the northern lights. (Later I learned their sightings might actually be true, not because I'm so special but because whenever anyone is in love or speaking of love or uplifted by joy and mantled in the Holy Spirit, the energy field flares up, shining with divinity.)

One day I asked my friend Anne Gehman if she could teach me to see auras.

Anne is a brilliant medium and the pastor at the Center for Spiritual Enlightenment in Washington, D.C. She has a summer house in Lily Dale, in southwestern New York, one hour south of Buffalo. Lily Dale, dating back to the 1880s, is perhaps the most celebrated center for spiritualism in the United States, a gated community jam-packed with psychics, spiritualists, and mediums.

In summer, visitors pay a ten-dollar fee to drive around the neat, trim, pastel and white–painted clapboard houses that surround a lovely lake, home to two swans, Lily and Dale. Here you can visit the pet cemetery and a grove of magnificent trees, where many a séance has been held. You can have your pick of readings from licensed psychics and mediums, and if you are not satisfied, they'll give your money back. There is a museum and a gracious 1890s hotel where, on the first floor, you may view the beautiful pastels that witnesses watched mysteriously appearing hour by hour on the canvas, apparently painted by a spirit hand.*

---

* During the nineteenth century, the heyday of spiritualism, spirits wrote on slates, drew pictures, rapped and tapped, tilted tables, moved objects around a room, and made their presence known in other exotic ways, including ectoplasmically. You hear less of these sensational appearances today. One medium I know says the reason is that earlier the spirits, attempting to get our attention, required dramatic effects that today are no longer necessary, but another reason may simply be that mediums, having learned to avoid adverse publicity, now offer such effects only in private séances and spirit circles. The nineteenth century saw plentiful charges of fraud to go along with these physical manifestations. Houdini uncovered the sleight-of-hand behind some of the rapping and writing. The Committee for Skeptical Inquiry, which issues *Skeptical Inquirer Magazine*, has interested itself in others. Recently it investigated the spirit paintings at Lily Dale and, unsurprisingly, found them to be frauds.

Just as a healer cannot heal himself but needs another
healer, so a psychic may have intuitions but often cannot
give a reading for herself.

ANNE IS A PROFESSIONAL PSYCHIC, dowser, and medium.
Oil companies have hired her to find deposits. Universities have
studied her gifts. The police have called her to find lost children
or solve a murder. She is a gentle woman, strong, resilient, and
private. She has known sorrow, betrayal, divorce, and difficulties,
for a psychic cannot always read for herself. She has been married twice and has both children and grandchildren—an ordinary
woman, except that she remembers her own birth and described
it to her mother with alarming accuracy, right down to what was
said in the delivery room and the color of the walls. One of eight
children, she has had her gifts since earliest babyhood, when she
could see entities and spirits moving among the people around
her. She was raised by Mennonite parents, became a nurse,
moved to Florida, left nursing to pursue her career as a trance
medium, and now lives in Springfield, Virginia. She is married
to an ex-Jesuit, Wayne Knoll, who teaches at prestigious Georgetown University in Washington, D.C. And she is a brilliant medium. Once, giving a reading to a Greek woman, she broke into
that language to report the words of the attendant spirit—and
she doesn't speak a word of Greek!

One day I was visiting at her summer place in Lily Dale.
"Can you teach me to see auras?" I asked her one afternoon as
we rocked in the white wicker chairs on the porch of her pretty
little pink-trimmed white house.

"Yes, but we have to wait till the light gets soft. It's easier to see when the light is even, not so bright."

A little later, as the dying sun cast long streamers across the lawns and a soft, sweet light permeated the air, Anne nodded to me.

"I think we could try it now," she said.

I straightened in anticipation and brought both feet to the deck. She was sitting upright in her chair against the pale boards of the house.

"What I want you to do is to squeeze your eyes tight shut, then open them and look a little to the side of my head *but with a soft focus*. Don't look right at my face. Look off to the side or above my head."

I shut my eyes tight, opened them, and saw a flash of colors surrounding her: purple, gold, pink, blue! But they were gone in an instant!

"Wow! Just for a minute."

"It takes practice. Try it again." She repeated the instructions. "Squeeze your eyes shut. Remember, soft focus, and don't look directly at me. Look a few inches to one side."

But this time something even more extraordinary happened.

"*Uh-oh.*" I shook my head.

"What is it?" she asked.

"I don't see your aura," I said, uncomfortable. "But, *um*, there's a man standing behind you."

"Oh." She was delighted. "What's his name? Ask him his name."

I think if she had doubted me even for one minute, I could not have continued, but it was so natural for her to hear about a spirit that I had no time to think.

I gave a name.

"That's my uncle." She nodded happily. "What else?" And before I knew it I was giving my first reading. When I finished, Anne praised me. "That's one of the best readings I've ever had. You're very talented."

I didn't believe her, and it was another five or six years before I dared to give another reading. I didn't understand mediumship, didn't feel altogether comfortable being one, and moreover (born with a healthy dose of skepticism) I had no interest in it.

What I wanted was to see auras.

Dream of your own beauty.

WALL GRAFFITI IN GUILDFORD, ENGLAND

How to See Auras

Some people *see* the energy, and others feel or *sense* it. I know one man who says he *smelled* the attar of roses and felt an aura whenever his avatar, Sai Baba, passed by in India. I should add that the saint Sai Baba lived from roughly 1835 to 1918 and at the time had certainly been dead (or had reached Mahasamadhi, as his disciples call it) for sixty years or more. My friend was staying in his ashram in India,* where Sathya Sai Baba (born Sathyanarayana Raju on November 23, 1926)

---

* Sai Baba taught no particular religion but loved both Islam and Hinduism. He advised his followers to lead a moral life, help others, love every living being without discrimination, treat all with love, and develop faith and patience. He criticized atheism. In his teachings Sai Baba emphasized the importance of performing one's duties without attachment to earthly matters and being ever content regardless of the situation. He taught that God penetrates and lives in every being, for God is the essence of all. He emphasized the complete oneness of God, a philosophy close to the Islamic *tawhid* and the Hindu Upanishads.

is said to be the reincarnation of the great saint, whose name he took. But now we're far from auras.

I myself find it easier to "see" an aura against a white or pale background (a wall is a good place to begin) and hardest against a patterned wallpaper or in harsh sunlight.

Try seeing the energy field when you are sitting in a group at a business conference, perhaps, or a committee meeting, with a number of people seated at a table. The light should be soft and even.

You can't be tense or in a competitive "thinking" state. (Therefore you must choose your meeting carefully: You don't want your boss to blindside you with a sudden request when you're busy looking for auras; but many a dull meeting requires only half your attention, leaving plenty of time for doodling.)

Choose a person across the table. Rest your eyes gently a few inches above or to one side of his head, or else at the triangle between the shoulder and head. Soften your focus. You may see colors shooting out, a flash of fire that is instantly gone. More likely at first you will see a shadow of light. I want to say a "white" light, but isn't light always colorless? And this colorless "shadow" does not disappear but becomes clearer as you gaze at it. Is it your imagination? Shift your eyes to the next person in the room and see if she, too, emits a corona of light. Shift to a third, and soon you will see that everyone in the room is encased in light.

It's important to keep your eyes softly focused. You are not "looking" or "staring" but idly observing the wall behind the individual.

If you have trouble seeing this play of light, shift your eyes a little farther from the person's head. An energy field extends anywhere from a few inches to two or three feet around the person, depending on the individual and his state of mind.

Play with it. Does one person have a larger energy field than another? Can you see it shining off the arms or legs? Does clothing interfere? Does the emotional state of the subject affect his aura, and if so, how? With a little practice you will see it all the time!

Remember, it requires a calm and receptive mind, the quiet intuitive state. If you are nervous, anxious, or stressed; if you are angry or feeling threatened; if you are working out a problem that has your mind churning with critical, analytical reasoning, don't even *try*.

Take your time.

Be gentle with yourself.

This is supposed to be fun.

WHAT DO AURAS have to do with intuition? When you see the aura, you are seeing into the very *essence* of the person. Seeing or sensing it changes not only the way you treat others but also the way you talk to yourself. You stop berating, scolding, and shaming yourself. You become more tolerant, more respectful of others (and yourself), and, in return, you find that they perceive and treat you differently as well.

As you develop awareness, you discover you can hold the

image of a person between your pulsing hands, fill yourself with light for three or four minutes, and then send healing energy *by intention alone* to the other person. She will feel it. Is this a sort of prayer, the prayer of touch? Healers do it all the time, of course, but the fact is that *anyone* can learn to send energy across time and space, just as anyone can influence a random-operating machine at the Princeton School of Engineering, even from the ends of the earth. In this case, however, it is not your own auric energy that you are sending forth on this knightly quest but rather the universal life force, the energy of love. Therefore, you don't pick up the diseases of others and neither do you pass on to others any hindrances or difficulties you may be going through yourself.

A friend was driving to work one day across Memorial Bridge toward the Lincoln Monument when the thought flashed into her mind: *What if I knew I had* everything?

Why, I could forgive them all! she thought.

Forgive yourself. Forgive the ones who hurt you. Be forgiven.

What would it feel like to know this? To know absolutely: *I am forgiven*. And, *I am*.

Skeptics will tell you this business of perceiving auras is nonsense. In one test, various psychics were asked to pick out people hidden behind a screen, the presumption being that their auras would shine above the screen. They couldn't do it.

SOME YEARS HAVE PASSED, and I know more about energy fields now, and why one person's aura will flare up high and wide, expanding bountifully, and why if you are ill or depressed or afraid, it shrinks back almost to your skin. The energy field that surrounds each person, together with the messages of hope that we receive from the Spiritual Dimension, stand as a perpetual reminder of who we are and where we are going and how we're doing along the way.

There is a beautiful story of some monks who lived long ago in a remote and crumbling monastery. The good years were over. No young novitiates. The few remaining monks were old, bitter, querulous, and spiteful. They quarreled. The abbot was so concerned for the continuity of his monastery that finally he took a mule and rode out to consult a holy hermit who lived a full day's journey away to ask how to restore harmony and attract new members. The hermit told the abbot he would pray on it and to come back in a week.

A week passed, and the abbot journeyed back to the hermit in his lonely retreat. "Tell your monks," said the holy man, "I have seen that one of them is Jesus Christ returned."

The abbot was astonished. One of his brothers was Christ returned to earth? In his own monastery? He went back with the news. But which one? No one knew. They began to treat each other with respect and the adoration that they would give to Christ himself. Quarreling ceased. The monastery became a place of such harmony, peace, and happiness that it attracted young novitiates, drawn to the wisdom and luminous serenity of the elder monks. The monastery flourished, rich in joy, because no one knew which monk was Christ. Perhaps it could be . . . *you*.

IF YOU ARE DEPRESSED or physically ill, your aura shrinks. It will be dark in places, fragile and hard to discern. On the other hand, whenever you fall in love, whenever you are filled with heart-singing happiness, whenever you are enraptured by beauty or overcome by mystical insight, your energy field flares up. You are shot with light. Others notice it, even if they can't put it into words.

Look at the young woman who has just fallen in love. She is shining. Her skin is pure, her eyes bright.

"You're so beautiful!" we say, startled by her as she enters the room. "What's happened to you? You must be in love!"

She is alive with heightened energy, with light.

Sometimes we don't recognize exactly what we're seeing, but we want to remain near her. If you have ever had the chance to sit in the presence of an enlightened soul, a lama or saint, or any of the spiritual giants who are "self-realized" (as we say) or "God-realized" (is there a difference?), you feel yourself affected. Merely being in the same room with such a person intensifies and purifies your energy field. His mind is wide. His heart is huge. His energy is strong and pure. He is "hooked up" with the Atman, Christ, Allah, Almighty God, the Holy Spirit, the Universal Principle—whatever you call this mystery of eternal, immutable, boundless love—and he transfers this energy to you, spirit to spirit, aura to aura, like the singing tuning fork that makes a second fork begin to ring. The poet Percy Shelley wrote of this:

> Nothing in the world is single;
> All things by a law divine
> In one another's being mingle.

WHAT IS IT THAT AFFECTS YOU? It is the enlightened master's love.

This is why we love to be in love. To talk of love. We pay money to see movies about love, to read about love. We love to be near someone who is in love, because it affects our own energy field so that we catch fire as well, feeling ourselves transported into a finer space. Surely this is the radiance that Christ poured forth with such intensity that the woman who had been bleeding for twelve years was made whole merely by stooping down to touch the hem of His robe. She bent in humility, awe, hope, and gratitude before His light and let her fingers brush His robe.

"Who touched me?" He asked, and His disciples laughed, because weren't they being jostled on all sides by the crowd. But Jesus had felt His energy field flow out into her, healing her.

Ambrose Worrall, the renowned Baltimore healer and aeronautical engineer, wrote in his book *The Gift of Healing* about how he'd pass his hands across a patient and heal a deformity (this took many sessions) or ease her pain.

"I would wait. An impulse would come to make 'passes' with my hands. I did not know why. But the impulse was too strong to ignore and I would heed it, raising my hands, moving them lightly over an arm, a shoulder. Sometimes my hand would stop at a certain point and the man or woman would say, 'Yes, that is it. That is where the pain is.' I would say a silent prayer. . . . Then once more, entirely by intuition or inspiration, I would know that I had done as much as I could."

WE SAY THAT God is light and God is love.

What we forget is that we, too, are composed of the spark of the Divine. The very cells of our bodies are formed of energy and light. We are beings of light, with godlike energy. The psychologist Abraham Maslow called it self-actualization. The person who is self-actualized or self-realized or God-realized has understood who he really is. He is consciousness of God.

I once had the privilege of interviewing the Dalai Lama, who modestly claims, by the way, that he is not fully enlightened. "Only a little bit." He holds two fingers close together. "I have *this* much," he says, collapsing with laughter. I've noticed that all enlightened people are bursting with laughter, their sheer happiness overflowing in unquenchable delight.

After the interview I began to shake violently, my very soul enlivened by his presence. Tears poured down my cheeks, and all I wanted—longed for with all my heart—was to serve others unselfishly, to bring others to a state of grace. Enlightenment. Fearless happiness. Such is the power that one energy field exerts upon another. And it goes beyond intuition or clairvoyance, or at least it somehow includes these paranormal abilities. For aren't we spiritual beings walking around in our light shields, merging and melding with one another by thought and energy?

Conversely, if you are in the presence of a person who is strong and charismatic but possessed by anger, fear, or insecurity, you feel yourself afflicted by that, too, this time in a harsh and darkening way. Perhaps his force field comes from the volcanic boiling of repressed anger—a survival mechanism, an emotion designed to protect him from further hurt and fear. If you come near, I promise, you will sense that discord. It may even attract you initially. It is seductive, leading you to feel powerful, engaged, superior. To someone else it may feel disordered, uncomfortable. If you are sensitive, you may wonder why you suddenly feel irritable, unsettled, even violent, ready to blow up at the next person to cross your path.

Or perhaps you feel his pain, as if you are being whipped by psychic barbed wire. This happens too. The Indian poet and visionary Indira Devi, while driving in a car, saw a farmer beating his ox in a field. She cried aloud in pain. When she reached home and undressed, she found her back was covered with the red welts of the farmer's whip, as if she had taken the place of the ox. That's how sensitive we are to what's going on around us. Usually, however, we aren't that conscious. Usually we don't recognize what's happening—that we've picked up the feelings and emotions of those around us. We're unaware that we need to *learn* somehow to establish and guard our boundaries. It doesn't occur to most of us to ask why we have a headache when in the presence of one person, why we feel exhausted when in the presence of someone who is depressed, why we feel covered in black cobwebs while listening to one angry radio host, or want to start a fight while enraged with another.

The energy of anger can be attractive. Quarrels break out. Crowds turn into mobs. Wars start. It's exciting. You feel *alive*.

Once I was introduced to a man who claimed to be the reincarnation of one of the apostles of Christ. My hostess was so impressed she almost genuflected, and it's true he exhibited an enormous energy field. But to me—I could hardly wait to get away, he felt so dark, disordered, so powered by ego and sneering arrogance. It was interesting to see our hostess made breathless by his energy.

WHEN SOMEONE IS ANGRY, his aura may flare out forcefully, for thought creates energy. You see it most clearly when the anger is not directed at you. Look for it when you're on the bus, in your office, in a café or bar. If you see a man with jaw-clenched anger, study how his light field shoots out in long, wild streamers. His energy stabs the air, attacking in sharp, daggerlike ribbons, and if you are sensitive you may step back, for you are being physically attacked.

Anger is often a disguise for fear. See if you can perceive the underlying hurt. See how the aura differs from that of someone operating out of love.

Some people don't see the energy but "feel" it instead in their own bodies. People who have been traumatized often don't know where their own porous boundaries end and those of another individual begin, and they are tormented by the energy and emotions of everyone around them. This is especially true of children, sponges for the emotions of others. When you learn to use the information, though, and to consider it a signal of intuition, you're way ahead. I know one therapist who *feels* in her own body what is going on in her client.

"What's going on in your stomach right now?" she asks gently, directing the client's attention to his own twisted gut.

"How did you know that?"

"I feel your pain in my own body."

The trained intuitive or sensitive person learns to be aware of which emotions belong to her and which to the person standing near. Often these intuitions concern the gut, and we may find that the belly is more connected to the rest of the world and to other people than we imagine.

In one study of five hundred subjects, 89 percent of women and 72 percent of men reported "often or frequently" experiencing gut feelings. Seventy-eight percent of skeptics also reported belly-brain intuitions, their stomach tied in knots.

ALL OF THIS WOULD BE of no importance, a parlor game, were it not for the implications of auras and energy fields and what they have to do with intuition and, indeed, with our very understanding of the nature of the world and what happens when we pass the shuttered gates of death. For that we turn in the next chapter to another aspect of what Saint Julian of Norwich called her knowings and showings.

nine

PLAYING WITH ENERGY

WELL, THERE'S NOTHING like practice and some practical, do-it-yourself, hands-on experience to make you aware of and comfortable with subtle energies. Here are a few ways to have some fun.

COMBING YOUR AURA

If you find yourself upset or disturbed, here is a simple way to restore balance.

Stand still. Take a breath and let it out. Pass your hands a few inches from your body, moving down your body from your head to your hips and, if you are terribly distressed, then all the way down to your feet.

Flick the energy off the palms of your hands. You will feel energized and centered.

You can also comb the aura of someone else. The only thing is, *you must always ask permission first*.

I remember one day being with a child who was so tired that he had a tantrum. I took him aside and told him, "It's all right. Don't worry. Everything's going to be okay." When his sobs subsided, I asked permission to do something to make him feel better. When he nodded through his tears, I passed my hands down his little body from head to feet. My hands were five or six inches away from him, perhaps a foot. My right hand brushed down the front of his body while my left hand brushed down the back. Then I combed his sides.

Instantly his tears dried up. He was back in his body, ready to face the world again. The entire operation took two seconds.

Combing your aura looks odd. Do it in private, or, if you're in a public place, go into the restroom where no one is watching. Otherwise, people will think you're nuts.

FEELING AN ENERGY BALL

Some people *feel* or *sense* the energy field rather than *see* it.

Again, take a moment to go deep inside. Scan your body. Exhale slowly and take a few moments to center yourself.

Close your eyes. Hold your hands two or three feet apart. Focus your attention on the palms of your hands, and slowly, s l o w l y move your two hands together with tiny pulsing motions. Keep your attention on the palms of your hands. At a certain point you may feel a kind of spongy quality between your hands. Pulse your hands lightly to test the sensation. If you open your eyes, you may find that your hands are quite far apart.

Close your eyes again. Now slowly, s l o w l y move your hands closer together. Don't be afraid to allow them to pulse or vibrate, but keep your attention on the skin of your palms. You will feel this sponginess become a kind of ball between your hands. Your hands may be a good foot or more apart.

But now that you have "caught" this ball of energy, play with it. Twist your hands to feel the ball in space. Is it the size of a volleyball? A basketball? A baseball?

This is your own energy field. Experiment with it. Try to toss it away. What did that feel like, and when you bring your hands back together do you still have the ball, or has it been "tossed" elsewhere?

RIBBONS AT YOUR FINGERTIPS

Some people say that they can see an aura best against a black background, but I find it easier to perceive it against a white or pale wall. Experiment to discover which you prefer.

Cup your hands loosely, fingertips touching. (Your thumbs don't need to touch.) Now, with softly focused eyes, slowly pull your fingertips apart and watch the widening space *between* your fingertips. You will see ribbons of light stretching between your fingertips; and if your gaze is gentle and trusting, you will see every finger and thumb surrounded by light.

Spread your fingers wide apart and look at the spaces between your fingers. Can you see your own light field?

At first you may find it hard to see. You're looking at the *spaces*, not the flesh. We're accustomed to looking with hard and penetrating eyes, and this requires an entirely different way of softly focused seeing. Some people may see the ribbons of light or energy and ascribe it solely to their imagination. They doubt and deny their very eyes. It comes as a shock! We aren't told that we live in a surround of light. Play with it. Try seeing it on other people, too.

WORKING WITH A PARTNER

If you have a partner or friend, here is another way to play with auras.

As in the previous exercise, press your fingertips together

loosely, but this time keep your eyes closed as you draw your fingers slowly apart.

When your fingertips are three or four inches apart, your friend says, "Stop." *Do not open your eyes.* Keep your attention on the tips of your fingers.

Your partner chops the air between your hands in a swift, cutting gesture: down, up, down.

Like a shiver, you will feel the curious and somewhat uncomfortable sensation of having your energy field cut in two.

Reverse, and try it on your partner.

PARTNERING BACK-TO-BACK

The next exercise is performed out of doors in an open space, a meadow or lawn.

Center yourself. Feel yourself inside your body.

Now stand back-to-back with your partner. Pause a moment, feeling the warmth of each other's back and making a "connection." Put your awareness on your back, your spine. At a certain moment ("Okay, ready?"), you each begin to walk forward, away from one another. As you move apart, remain focused on your back. Can you still feel your partner's energy? After a few paces, stop, and *without turning around*, check your connection. Can he feel you? Can you feel him?

If so, walk on. If you lose the connection—cannot feel him— go back and start again.

Keep your focus on your back. How far apart can you move before you lose the connection?

PLAYING WITH PING-PONG BALLS

This next test also requires a partner, but this should be a special lover or good friend, for this exercise leads to surprising intimacy.

You both sit comfortably. Relax. Your eyes are open. You feel calm and easy. Place the palm of your hand against one of his. You don't need to squeeze your two hands tight, but the fingertips as well as the pads at the wrist should lightly touch. No pressure. No tension.

Allow your fingertips to rest together for a moment, making contact.

Focus your awareness on the palm of your hand.

Close your eyes.

Now s l o w l y pull your hands apart, two inches, three, four, always focusing on the skin at the palm of your hand and "listening" to the connection between you. Move very slowly.

At a certain point you will feel a ball of energy passing back and forth between you, like a Ping-Pong ball. *Pock! Pock! Pock!*

Sometimes, instead of the rally back and forth, it may feel like double *pocks,* in which the energy hits both hands simultaneously.

If you cannot feel it, move your hands farther apart, for the energies between you may be so strong that they go right *through* your hands without your catching them.

How far apart can you hold your hands and still feel the pulse of your partner's energy?

To end and cut the connection, slide your hands together and release.

You can also try this same exercise with your own two hands.

HEIGHTENING ENERGY

Just as you can *calm* your energy field by passing your hands *down* your body, you can also give energy to yourself or to another person by *lifting* the energy field or zipping *up*. Starting at the hips or trunk of the body, move your hands up the energy field toward the heart, the throat, the head. At the crown of the head, close your two hands together. Finished.

A word of warning: If you wish to give energy to a child who is tired or angry, holding himself in with all his strength, be careful. Heightening energy at this moment might be the straw that sends him into total collapse. It might be better, instead, to calm him with a *downward* pass of your hands.

BALANCING CHAKRAS
(OR HAVE YOU HAD ENOUGH?)

According to traditional Indian medicine, the chakras are great wheels of energy that whirl clockwise at seven major centers in the body. If someone you know is upset or distraught, balancing the chakras is an immediate way to bring her back to center, packing her energy field around her. It takes only one minute.

Stand on her right side, so that your right hand is at the front of her body, your left hand at the back.

Keeping your hands eight to twelve inches from her body, place them in the air first at the root chakra, located at the base of the spine. Your left hand hovers at the tailbone, low down the back, while your right hand is held an equal distance away from the pubic bone. Hold them there, listening, until you "catch" the ball of energy in both hands and feel it pulsing back and forth. (The root chakra is the hardest to catch, for when someone is upset he's usually up in his head, with little grounding energy. If you absolutely cannot feel it, move to the second chakra.)

When you've caught the root chakra energy, move your hands up to the second chakra, at the belly, and then continue up the body, pausing at each chakra until you feel the connection: third chakra at the solar plexus, fourth chakra at the heart, fifth chakra at the throat, sixth chakra at the brow. By the third chakra you should feel the energy strongly in both hands, for most people are "up in their heads."

When you finish at the brow, or sixth chakra, keep your left hand at the back of the head, but move your right hand from the brow to above the crown of the head, the seventh chakra. Hold it there. Feel the *ping* of energy in both hands.

You are almost finished.

Now to conclude: Holding your right hand above the crown, move your *left* hand down the person's back, pausing at each chakra to feel the connection between the crown and the lower chakras. Feel it *ping* in your hands.

When your left hand reaches the first or root chakra, your *right* hand moves from the crown of the head *down the back of the body* to meet your left hand at the buttocks.

Close your palms together and step away.

During this process, the person on whom you are working may feel a tingling in her hands as you are balancing her. If her eyes are closed, she may not be able to stop swaying back and forth.

Afterward, centered again, she will feel energized and strong, ready to tackle life anew.

Inviting Intuition III: Automatic Writing

I want to add here, for no reason other than intuitive associative thinking, another way to increase your intuition. It has many names, but I call it automatic writing. It's a way of talking to your Higher Self, your soul, protecting angels, if you will, and to hear the intuitions that are sometimes so fragile they cannot break through the layers of logic to bubble into consciousness. It presumes belief in a spiritual dimension and in some force that is guarding and loving you, but you may try it without any such conviction. In that case, you are speaking to your inner wisdom, your center, your psyche, or soul.

You may do this exercise either with a pencil or on a computer.

Begin by going into a light meditation. Relax. Let out your breath and allow yourself to enter a slightly altered state.

Sit up with your back straight, feet flat on the floor, and eyes closed.

You should be easy, comfortable, your head balanced on the column of your neck. Scan your body; wherever you feel tension send an invitation to that part of your body to relax, release the tension. This is especially true of the yoke we carry across our shoulders. Relax your shoulders, relax your facial muscles, relax your neck. . . .

When you feel still, begin with an invocation to your guides, or to God, an offering to your Higher Self, your inner wisdom. You will find your own words, but it might go something like:

O God, angels, guardian spirits: Come to me. Help me. Talk to me. Let me be open to your words. Speak to me, and let me hear you easily.

Perhaps you begin with a question that is puzzling you. Write the question down. Pause now. Listen. If you are using a pen or pencil allow your hand to drop to the page. I find myself, eyes closed, heart open, making small V's or M's at the top of the page, until the words spring telepathically to my mind. If you are at the computer, wait. Soon your fingers will begin to type. And now you'll find yourself writing things you never thought about before. Sometimes you'll use words not in your vocabulary.

Now ask your questions, all of them. Write down the answers, not because you may forget them but because these are beyond our normal everyday ideas.

Now you may have a dialogue with your Higher Self. The higher and more spiritual the questions that you ask, the higher the angel or guiding spirit writing through you, and you will *feel* its energy.

One day while engaged in such a practice, I asked, "Who are you? Is this just my imagination that I'm writing to? Show me!"

Instantly they left. I say "they," and yet I don't know if it was one Presence (as I suspect) or many, myself or a *fravashi*, an angel, a guide. But in a flash, I found myself alone in my body, pathetic, impotent, weak, and vulnerable.

Oh, the horror of that emptiness!

When only minutes earlier I had felt mantled in a warmth and comfort I hadn't even recognized, and now it was gone.

"Come back!" I called. I wanted that energy encasing me, the Light. And so tenderly does the Other Dimension care for us that instantly it returned. The creative writer or artist feels this same sensation when uplifted by the Muse. The athlete experiences this same sweet transport when in the zone. It is the Zen of tennis or archery or golf or Chinese calligraphy. It is the union of the mystic, yours at any time.

ten

MIND-SIGHT, OR WHAT IS CONSCIOUSNESS AND WHERE DOES IT GO WHEN WE DIE?

All analytical thought bows in silence
before the majesty of insight and the
touch of the spiritual dimension.

ANONYMOUS

IN 1846, JEAN-EUGÈNE ROBERT-HOUDIN, the most renowned magician of his time (the man from whom Harry Houdini would later take his name), asked for leave to investigate the claims of the amazing French clairvoyant Alexis Didier, who was astonishing all of Europe with his gifts. With bandaged eyes Didier could beat his opponent at a game of cards, knowing all the cards dealt, not only those in his own hand but also those in the hand of his antagonist. He claimed it was merely intuition. Or second sight. With his eyes closed, he could read pages selected at random in a book. He could describe a villa hundreds of miles away, down to the paintings on the wall.

It is widely accepted that it takes a fraud to uncover one. Robert-Houdin, knowing the magic tricks of conjuring and sleight-of-hand, asked to investigate the impostor. With his own hands he bandaged Didier's eyes, and when they were well encased in wadding and bandages, he took out two new decks of cards, still in their government-stamped wrappers, opened them, shuffled, asked Alexis to cut, and proceeded to play *écarté* against the blindfolded intuitive.

"You needn't pick up your hand," Alexis Didier said. "I take every trick."

"Let us begin again."

Again Didier took all the tricks.

A discomforting game. Each time the cards were dealt, Didier knew all the cards facedown.

Baffled, Robert-Houdin moved on to another test. He removed Didier's useless bandages, pulled a book from his pocket, and, indicating a particular starting place, asked him to read at a point that was eight pages farther on. Alexis pricked the page two-thirds down with a pin, returned the book to Houdin, and spoke: "*Après cette triste cérémonie. . . .*"

"Enough!" said Robert-Houdin, triumphant. He'd caught him! There were no such words on the eighth page, but after turning the page to the ninth, Houdin read at the same height, "*Après cette triste cérémonie. . . .*"

Robert-Houdin then drew out a letter. "Can you tell me who wrote this letter?"

Alexis Didier held the letter to the crown of his head and against his stomach. He made little mistakes describing the writer—the color of the hair was wrong, for example; and, seeing the letter writer surrounded by books, he called him a librarian, but Robert-Houdin ignored these trifling errors.

"Where does he live?"

Alexis described the house easily.

"Since you can see the house, what street is it on?"

"Give me a pencil," said Didier, and in a few minutes he gave the exact address, including the house number and street name.

"It is too much!" cried the investigating magician. "It's beyond me. One more word. What is the writer doing at this moment?"

"Be on your guard," said Didier. "He is betraying your confidence at this very moment!"

"Oh, that's an utter mistake. He's one of my best and most trusted friends."

"Take care."

"Nonsense!"

A year later Robert-Houdin discovered that his friend had defrauded him of 10,000 francs at the very time of the sitting.

Some time later Robert-Houdin returned to play another game of *écarté* against the clairvoyant. Each time Alexis Didier knew every card, often before it had been dealt.

"I left this séance then," wrote Robert-Houdin in testimony, "in the greatest possible state of amazement, and convinced of the utter impossibility of chance or conjuring having been responsible for such marvellous results."

> If Contemplation which introduces us to the very heart of creation does not inflame us with such love that it gives us, together with deep joy, the understanding of the infinite misery of the world, it is a vain kind of contemplation; it is the contemplation of a false God. The sign of true contemplation is charity. By the capacity for forgiveness shall I recognize your God and also your opening to creation.
>
> MARIUS GROUT, French Quaker

WHAT IS CONSCIOUSNESS? How can the mind o'erleap its physical senses and move into realms remote to eye and ear? And if it can, then where or *when* does this awareness end?

I'm fascinated by what happens to us when we die. I'm not afraid of dying (though terrified of the pain that may accompany it; horrified also at the prospect of becoming a burden to my children, an Alzheimer's vegetable "sans teeth, sans eyes, sans taste, sans everything," including continence and, most important, consciousness, by which I mean awareness of what is happening around me, of the glass of water at my hand, the light in the soap bubbles in the kitchen sink, the faces of my beloved children and their kids). I accept without question the reality of intuition, telepathy, premonitions, presentiment, and psychic or paranormal experiences. I accept also the concept of spirits and invisible guardians watching over us, of angels and a spiritual medium in which we live like fish in water, and later in this book I will speak about sensitives and psychics and the difference between them and the mediums who see spirits and ghosts. Meanwhile, I keep tight hold for the moment on this topic of intuition in its narrowest sense. What's interesting about precognition and intuition and other forms of *psi* is the number of people who believe they've had at least one experience. Present understanding of our brains leaves no room for these phenomena.

SOMETIMES AS I'M GOING to bed at night, I ask for the solution to a problem that's been puzzling me, for I have learned the ancient folk wisdom of "Sleep on it. You'll know the answer in the morning." Like many people, I keep a pad of paper by the bed and a pen or pencil in order to write down dreams and nighttime insights.

On this particular occasion I'd been noodling on intuition, wondering if there is a special spot in the brain for intuition and psychic abilities. I asked that night to be shown the truth, that is, to have a demonstration of how intuition works.

My dream was vivid, realistic, which is one of the signs of a "gifted dream," for some dreams are nothing but the busy mind emptying the day's trash into the dumpster. But this dream was lucid, colorful, memorable.

I saw the inside of my brain, and lights, which I knew were thoughts, sweeping like tidal waters washing through a sponge— pouring in and out, over and through the cells of my brain, and not just lighting up one segment of my brain (as I'd imagined) but all the areas except one. In my dream I tried to express what I was seeing, to describe it, but the language center (which, in my dream was at the left side of my temple—the left parietal) was mute; and in the dream I understood that if language were activated, the wash of intuition (at least in my dream) could not be discerned.

These intuitions could be expressed later, but the bolt from the blue comes, like mystical union, empty of words. Lights flare up throughout the brain, flashing here and there, but the "knowing" arrives visually, as in a painting or else accompanied by physical sensations such as goose bumps, chills, hairs rising on your scalp or neck, a wrenching in the gut, or your feet racing out of danger. But for that instant, language, cognition, is deliberately cut off. Why? In my dream I knew the reason was to force me to *listen!* and respond without "thinking" through the facts.

Was my dream a true depiction of intuition and heightened and psychic abilities at work? I don't know. When monks, nuns, and experienced meditators are hooked up to brain scan machines during intense prayer and meditation, it is the prefrontal cortex that lights up, while the parietal area goes dark, as the meditators tap into the transcendent, speechless silence of unity with the Divine. The prefrontal cortex is known as the seat of cognition, intellect, reasoning. The left parietal controls language (just as I saw!); the right parietal is concerned with nonverbal memory.

A WOMAN SAT in her car at the red light. It turned green.

"You can go," her daughter said.

Still she sat. "I think I'll stay," she thought, not knowing why, and curiously the cars on her left also didn't move. Suddenly a car raced into the intersection, plunged through the red light, and tore around the corner. Had she moved when the light turned green, that car would have killed her daughter in the passenger seat.

How did she know to wait?

I'm told that Winston Churchill escaped a bomb one day by uncharacteristically taking a different seat than usual.

Lyn Buchanan, who worked for the U.S. military as a controlled remote viewer and who later founded a company that teaches pathways to inner intuition, was waiting in his car one evening to cross a busy two-lane highway when suddenly, as if with a mind of its own, his car leaped across the steady stream of commuter traffic, dodged between the oncoming cars, and landed safely on the far side just as a truck plowed into the post where seconds earlier he'd been waiting in his car. Intuition? Foresight? Second sight? Precognition?

Nobel laureate Eric R. Kandel, professor and director of the Kavli Institute for Brain Science at Columbia University, who performed prizewinning experiments on marine snails, admitted in a personal e-mail: "We know little about the brain mechanisms of consciousness or intuition."

To a degree it does not lend itself to scientific investigation. According to the Dalai Lama (and Buddhism has been investigating consciousness for millennia), the nature of consciousness or awareness, *shepa* in Tibetan, has no material form or shape at all. Instead of having some material nature, consciousness is "mere experience" or "awareness."

But is that all? Some years ago neuroscientists thought the neurons in the brain couldn't change or regenerate. Now we know that the brains of London cabbies grow huge simply by their having to learn every street and avenue and alleyway in that huge city. Birds learn to peck a hole in the paper top of milk bottles so they can drink the milk. People who meditate change the very structure of their brains, opening access to the deep gamma waves that are then paramount. By meditating they heal physiological breaches in the brain.

A case study reported in 1980 in *Science* concerned a hydrocephalic student at Sheffield University, England, who had virtually *no brain*! Increased intracranial pressure had compressed his cerebral cortex against his skull to less than a millimeter in thickness. Nonetheless, he had an IQ of 126 and graduated with first-class honors in mathematics.

And we think we know anything about consciousness?

We observe the physical world around us and name it "consciousness," but without experience we'd forget the outer world we're looking at. Memory plays its part in consciousness by enabling us to recall our own experiences or be aware of emotions surging through us; and all of this we think of as basic consciousness. Yet there's still another, even higher aspect of consciousness: the "luminous quality of the mind" that shines on the external world and sees it not as separate from itself but integral. The idea of separation is itself a trick of consciousness. Indeed, how can the conscious mind look into or study itself?

The fact is, we're hard put even to say when someone is conscious or not. Witness the controversy over Terri Schindler Schiavo, who was in a persistent vegetative state (PVS) for fifteen years, until she was allowed to die by court order in 2005. Was she "alive"? Did she know what was happening around her? Could she hear and think? Was she *dead* before they shut down the machines that kept her heart beating, her lungs taking in air?

> At one time "locked-in" patients were thought to be un-
> conscious. However, those who have brain function but
> cannot communicate because of brain injury may have a
> new way to make their needs known. Engineers at the Uni-
> versity of Toronto have developed a system that measures
> blood flow to the parts of the brain that process prefer-
> ences. If it works, it will allow patients to express a choice
> and have that decision understood.

In 2006 the *Journal of Clinical Investigation* published new research on the recovery of Terry Wallis, who lived nineteen years in a minimally conscious state (MCS). In 1984, as a nineteen-year-old, Terry survived a car crash that sheared the nerve connections in his brain, putting him in a minimally conscious state and rendering him quadriplegic. His parents visited regularly, talking to him all the time, until one day, nineteen years later, he spoke the word *Mom,* and so began his recovery.

This has added to the growing evidence that with therapy those with "hopelessly" severe brain injuries may be able to recuperate. And it throws into question everything we know about consciousness, awareness, life itself.

Because human consciousness must involve both pleasure and pain. To strive for pleasure at the exclusion of pain is, in effect, to strive for the loss of consciousness.

ALAN WATTS

Time after time, a patient dies on the operating table, brain waves flat, no pulse or vital signs, only to recover a few minutes (in at least one case *hours!*), later to report on what happened during the lapse: the surgeons' conversations, the efforts to bring the patient back to life. Raymond Moody wrote of this phenomenon as long ago as 1975 in his book *Life After Life*, followed by further reports by Kenneth Ring, professor emeritus in psychology at the University of Connecticut, and by so many others that today the acronym NDE or "near-death experience" has become as commonly recognized as "out-of-body" experience. Betty Eadie wrote about what happened in her near-death experience in her book *Embraced by the Light,* and Dannion Brinkley claims to have been killed not once but thrice, revealing tales of a dark tunnel, a crystal city, a cathedral of knowledge, and angels offering revelations of the future. The 1982 near-death experience of Mellen-Thomas Benedict, who "died" of cancer, echoes the others, with the Light pulling him into one experience after another and shifting into images of Christ, the Buddha, mandalas, archetypical images, Lord Krishna, and his Higher Self. He drank of the River of Life. He visited pre-Creation before the Big Bang and stood in the mystic's void of absolute, pure consciousness, in the energy and vibration of the space between atoms. And later, when he was brought back once more into "the vibratory realm," as he called it, he tasted the gift of "being the human part of God." He had been declared clinically dead and remained so, we're told, for an hour and a half.

One of the most compelling and verifiable stories concerns a girl, Vicky Bright, who "died" in a car crash. She woke up hovering at the ceiling of an operating room and from that vantage point observed the surgeons working on her cloth-draped body below.

"Well," said one, "she may not even survive. And if she does, she could be in a permanent vegetative state." An upsetting thought.

Later, when she came back in her body and was recovering from the surgery, she reported everything she had heard and seen—the brilliant colors, the lights, the words spoken, the actions taken, her own shaved hair, the wedding ring on her hand, and none of this would have been remarkable if you believe that consciousness continues after death, *except that Vicky had been blind from birth*.

Kenneth Ring calls it *mind-sight*, a kind of spiritual sense.

The curious case of Pam Reynolds offers another view of how boundless is our consciousness. Her full story was written up in Michael Sabom's book *Light and Death,* and retold by NPR reporter Barbara Bradley Hagerty in her beautiful *Fingerprints of God*, but it doesn't mean the events should not be retold here, so powerful are the implications of this oneiric quality of the human brain.

When she was thirty-five Pam had a basilar artery aneurysm, with blood leaking into her brain. She flew to Arizona for "standstill" surgery. There the doctors taped her eyes shut, packed her body in ice to lower her temperature, and stopped her heart. When her temperature dropped to about 60 degrees, the doctors drained all the blood out of her body, so that the aneurism sac in her brain would collapse and could be clipped.

At that point she had no pulse, no blood pressure, no respiration, no brain activity. Technically she was not alive. After the operation, the surgeons warmed the blood, transfused it into her body, and, at about 78 degrees, started Pam's heartbeat again.

But from Pam's point of view what happened was remarkable. As with many NDEs, she reported floating to the ceiling and looking around with intense awareness. It was wonderful! Colors were extravagant, sounds intensified, and all her senses sharper than in life. She watched the doctors working on her body—and didn't care. She heard their words, examined with curiosity the

surgeon's drill, and at that moment saw a pinprick of light calling
to her. She felt herself pulled toward the light, and there stood
her grandmother and her musician uncle, David Saxton, who had
died earlier of a heart attack. Behind them stood a sea of people,
all shimmering with light and looking young and joyous and beautiful, and wearing "coats of light."

"Is God the light?" she asked, and the answer came back
telepathically: "No. . . . The light is what happens when God
breathes."

"When God breathes," she thought, riven by joy. "I am standing in the breath of God."

Pam stood in the breath, yearning to dive deeper into the
Light, when her uncle David informed her that she had to go
back into her body. She didn't even want to *look* at her body. She
protested, refused, and then her uncle *pushed* her. "And I hit the
body, and I heard the title track to the Eagles' album *Hotel California*. When I hit the body the line was: 'You can check out
anytime you like, but you can never leave.'" After she recovered,
she thought she'd been hallucinating, despite the fact that her
deepest brain functions had been shut off. But a year later, when
she described what she had seen and heard of the surgery in the
operating room, her doctor confirmed it all. And what does this
say about consciousness? Or death?

Frequently it's a family member who greets the one who has
"died." When my friend Sonia's son Carl died in a car accident,
it was his grandfather who met him in the Light and sent him
back into his broken body.

SOMETHING LIKE EIGHT MILLION PEOPLE have had a near-
death experience (NDE). In other words they clinically died
(evidencing no brain or heart activity) and mysteriously returned

to life. (But they did not really die, did they? Or they'd not be back giving reports.) Some saw nothing: the River Lethe of forgetfulness. But many return with tales of encountering a great light or beautiful Beings of Light, often perceived as sheer Intelligence. Some were met by angels and sages, others by dead relatives welcoming them. One child who returned from this chthonic journey told his father he had met a "little brother," at which the father burst into tears and confirmed that, yes, an older baby had died before this boy was born.

These blessed souls, returning, also uniformly report knowing that everything in the Universe operates perfectly, according to a perfect plan, even suffering, even famine, torture, war, abuse. Even our unanswered prayers. Often these individuals are transformed by their experience. They have had a spiritual awakening. They can no longer tolerate the physical world with its illusions, anger, materialism, its polarities of judging everything as good/bad, black/white, either/or, we/they. Nothing appears to them as before, and they are not quick to decide anymore what's good for us or bad but only *what is.*

IT WAS WHILE THINKING about this book that I began to wonder how truly odd is consciousness. We think. We respond to neural stimuli (pokes, punches, pricks). We have sudden flashes of intuition—"Don't move!"—that sometimes save our lives. And roughly every sixteen or seventeen hours, every adult, child, and doddering aged creature lies down and goes to sleep. Soldiers in opposing armies put down their weapons, turn out the lights, and fall asleep. Bankers, builders, beggars and brawlers, dictators and prisoners, pacifists and terrorists, mothers and babies—everyone gives pause to conscious cognition and drops into a state of otherness. We dream. We live alternative states in sleep and then wake up and wind up the mortal coil again.

Consciousness is marked by creativity, intuition, the play of imagination. We see its operation not only in the beating of a heart, the pulsing orange or green line of an electrical brain monitor, the rise and fall of breath, digestion and defecation, but also in eye movements and our cries of joy and pain. We see it in hearts broken by grief or in the entanglement of telepathy and precognition, in clairvoyance and remote or distant viewing.

One man I know went to a psychic who told him that his great-grandmother Julia was there, pleased to see him. He went home to his mother.

"I didn't know I had a great-grandmother Julia."

"Oh, don't be silly. Of course you do. I've told you about her!"

I REMEMBER MY MOTHER telling me while riding in the car with her (I remember the very crossroad that we passed, such an impression did her words make on me as a child) that when you die "your life passes before your eyes." Folktales are rich with such reports. People have been dying and returning, apparently, since the beginning of time.

You see your life like a movie flashing before your eyes, she told me, and events are shown dispassionately and without judgments of good or bad (no punishment). Rather, you see them from the point of view of everyone involved. I read of one child who decided to come back to life because during this review she understood that she was being shown only those moments when she "hadn't loved enough." She returned to life in order to love more deeply this time around. Is compassion another aspect of consciousness?

And here's another question: Does consciousness include our character or personality? People who experience NDEs retain their personality. Think of that! They met beloved parents, angels, and deities.

So it's not goodbye when we die but sayonara, hasta la vista, see ya, I'll meet you over there. Swedenborg has a lot to say about what happens when we die, and how those who have lived good lives go to a place of goodness, and those who have lived evil lives also go there but find themselves so uneasy in heaven that gladly they flee to the hell of their own making and comfort level.

Meanwhile, what can we do to increase our intuition, creativity, and heightened perceptions? Our consciousness? What can we do to *awaken* and enter the luminous mystery that so often we approach with dulled eyes and plodding footsteps? The answer lies in our brain waves, and this, too, as you see in the next chapter, is a skill that can be learned.

eleven

MIND MIRROR & MIND-FLOW

*You need not do anything. Remain sitting
at your table and listen. Just wait. And
you need not even wait, just become
quiet and still and solitary. And the world
will offer itself to you to be unmasked. It
has no choice. It will roll in ecstasy at
your feet.*

FRANZ KAFKA

ONE EVENING, while I was at a busy Washington fund-raising reception, the buzz of voices rising around me and the milling crowd pressing around tables piled with food and drinks, a friend approached, and, shouting over the noise, asked what was going on these days. It is one of the laws of the Universe that you don't really have to *do* anything. Just notice what you want and watch it rush into your arms.

"I've been wondering what Consciousness is," I answered. "I need someone who knows how the brain works."

"Oh, you need to meet George Pierson," she cried. "He teaches people to work with their brains. Look, there's my son. He knows how to reach George. Let me introduce you."

And that's how I found myself a few weeks later in a spectacular penthouse in Silver Spring, Maryland, with views from the wraparound terrace across the Rock Creek woodlands to the Washington Monument and the Capitol, and toward the west over a canopy of treetops to the commercial, high-rise towers of Rockville, Maryland, miles away.

George Pierson is a hearty, rumpled man with that daring eccentricity that marks the creative mind, and his apartment revealed his eclectic interests: the plants on the sunstruck terraces, the candles and flowers placed at the feet of the gargantuan statue of the Buddha that dominated the entrance hall, the spare, masculine black and grey lines of his living room, and a modern kitchen with granite counters laden with shiny machines waiting to grate, grind, blend, or boil as required. But the most impressive feature to me were the two rooms set aside for a terrifying array of computers, lamps, TVs, stereos, and brain-wave machines, all joined by electric cords black-snaking over the floors and around the chairs. This is a man who loves technology.

In 1979 George worked in the promotion department of HBO, where he became fascinated with the creative process and also with what his mind seemed able to do. If two people in his department were fighting, for example, he discovered he could go home that evening, sit quietly, send them harmonious thoughts, and the next morning their quarrel would have been resolved. Such things happened often enough for him to begin to ask: Did his *intention* have something to do with this? Was the harmony he tried to project actually affecting them?

In 1994 Discovery TV recruited him for senior vice president in creative promotion. His task was to inspire creativity, and he started playing with the question of why some people are more creative than others, and its corollary: Can genius be taught?

> Intuition is a natural state, like breathing, and the only time
> you inhibit it is by addiction to drugs or alcohol, mind-
> altering substances intended to induce power but which
> instead disrupt the wisdom of the mind.

It was at Discovery that he met Anna Wise, the leading brain-wave practitioner of her time. Author of several books, Wise studied under the British scientist and Zen master Maxwell Cade, considered the father of biofeedback in England. Cade was interested in measuring the brain-wave patterns of people in higher states of consciousness, and he developed, in conjunction with Geoffrey Blundell, an EEG designed to measure only consciousness. They named it the Mind Mirror.

In 2003, Pierson received his certification after successfully completing Anna Wise's program of Creative Mind-Flow for Better Brains, and says he has helped more than one thousand people become more creative and more intuitive through brain-wave training. Indeed, to have the *Aha!* experience *on demand!* Anna Wise calls this the Awakened Mind, which is what the Buddha called it, too.

"Are you Enlightened?" the Buddha was asked. He answered, "I am Awake."

Pierson challenges the idea that some people are more intuitive than others. He says that once you learn to maintain an open flow of information between the conscious and subconscious minds, *you can enter these creative states at will.* With training, he says, everyone can learn to use all brain-wave frequencies. Everyone can enter altered states of awareness and demonstrate what we call genius.

The first thing he did was settle me in his living room and make a formal PowerPoint presentation of what he calls mind-flow.

Energy follows Thought, he instructed. Thought directs Energy. Thought or Intention has physical power.

The Energy of Thought

So many studies have been done on the effect of thought or intention on plants and lower animal forms (snails, shrimp) that you wouldn't think anyone needed to test it any longer. Talking to plants in loving kindness makes them thrive. Sending prayer or loving intentions to petri dishes of microbes or blood plasma or seedlings makes the microbes, red blood cells, or seedlings grow faster than those in a control group with no exposure to kindly thoughts.

The visionary and creative Japanese researcher Dr. Masaru Emoto alleges that the energy of thoughts, words, and music affects the molecular structure of water, which he documents by freezing droplets of water and photographing them under a dark-field microscope.

His book *The Hidden Messages in Water* shows the twisted, distorted drop of water that formed under the thought "You make me sick," and the exquisite crystals that formed when soothed with "I love you" and "Thank you." Dirty and polluted water in a vial became clean when bombarded with generous thanks and loving intentions, while clean water barraged with hateful words turned ugly.

Should this surprise us? Aren't we, too, influenced by a soft voice and a generous aspect? "A soft answer turneth away wrath," goes the ancient proverb, as exemplifed in the folktale of the North Wind and the Sun competing to see which could make a man remove his coat.

For over thirty years an office at the Princeton Engineering Anomalies Research (PEAR) program has demonstrated the effect of Intention (or Thought) on random-operating machines. You sit in front of one of a number of machines and *send an intention for* the machine to behave in a particular fashion, and according to PEAR the machines respond at statistically significant levels. One machine is a fountain of water, and your task is to make the water shoot higher or lower, or wider or thinner. Another is a computer with a variety of pictures randomly appearing on the screen; you try to bring up the cheetah (or pyramid or city) more often than others. There is a box that spews out random numbers, which you direct to spike high or drop low. There is a round table with a robot on the center, and you try by thought alone to move the robot in one direction or another of the compass rose.

Distance makes no difference. You can send your intention from Australia to the machine in Princeton, and your intention registers at statistically significant levels.

Time makes no difference. You can send your intention ten days early, and statistically significant results occur. Moreover, you can send your intention *after the machine has made its run,* and if the data have not yet been reviewed and recorded, the machine will have registered the postdated intention. Imagine! The past is malleable to Thought!

Two people working together have twice the effect of a single individual on the machines. Two people who are in love with each other—and I mean erotic, passionate, romantic, sexual love—have *seven* times the effect. Negative emotions such as anger, jealousy, and vengeance have no effect. Apparently what affects random-operating, non-organic matter is the energy of compassion, delight, and joyful love.

THE BRAIN PRODUCES electrical impulses all the time that have both frequency and amplitude. The amplitude shows the power of the impulse, as measured in microvolts. The frequency is the speed of these waves, measured in cycles per second (hertz), and there are four frequencies: beta, alpha, theta, and delta. (The reason that beta comes first in this list instead of second, as in the Greek alphabet from which the terms are taken, is because the lower alpha waves were the first to be discovered, and only later were the higher frequencies of beta found. Too late; the terms could not be changed.)

Your state of consciousness arises from the fluid combination of these four frequencies, and a person with the creative and intuitive "awakened" mind is using all four in symphonic harmony. (A fifth, the mysterious gamma wave, is found in spiritually evolved lamas and spiritual giants when they are meditating, but mindflow is not concerned with these, but rather with helping ordinary people to discern and utilize the more common frequencies.)

Beta waves (38–15 hertz) are what most people use most of the time. When you're in Times Square bombarded by stimuli, alert, analyzing and negotiating life, you're using beta frequencies. Beta waves are associated with logical thinking, problem solving, heightened sensitivity. Too much beta, however, and you can't stop worrying; your mind races; your heart pounds; you are plagued by anxiety, restlessness, and sleepless nights.

Classical music, especially that of Mozart, throws your brain waves into the lower frequencies of creativity and intuition. Hard rock, on the other hand, sets off tsunamis of brain waves that smash against each other violently.

Curiously, using a cell phone interrupts beta waves and makes you spacey. This is why driving a car while talking on your cell phone is doubly dangerous, not only because it splits your attention but also because even while looking straight at an oncoming truck your distorted beta brain-wave frequencies can't compute the coming accident. You see the truck and cannot respond.

Beta waves are vital to the creative process but only in conjunction with the three lower frequencies: alpha, theta, and delta.

Alpha waves vibrate at from 14 to 9 hertz, slower than beta. With alpha you have a relaxed, detached, receptive air. The five senses are associated with alpha, as is the ability to process them: to recognize sights, sounds, smells, taste, touch. In alpha everything takes on a sacred and holy radiance, for Nature itself vibrates at a frequency equivalent to alpha. Being in nature, therefore, throws you into alpha. You are using alpha waves when gardening or walking in nature, when watching a waterfall, when aimlessly daydreaming. Tests of intuition and ESP indicate an increase of alpha waves. For most people the problem is not having too much alpha but not enough. Alpha is the bridge between the conscious and subconscious mind. Without alpha you can't remember your theta dreams, even when they are vivid, important.

Below alpha, the slower theta waves vibrate at from 8 to 5 hertz. This is the arena of the subconscious and of long-term memory. In theta you find suppressed and psychological material locked deep in the caverns of the psyche. Enhanced by amplitude, theta is the frequency of high-functioning creativity and intuition. You are flooded with energy. Theta changes feelings into poetic metaphors of colors, shapes, sound. It offers us the poetry of the unconscious. In theta you are moved by empathy and compassion, overwhelmed by the gallantry of the human race. Then, with Miranda in *The Tempest*, you exclaim, "O Brave New World / that has such people in't."

In theta you experience bursts of insight—the bolt from the blue that cuts through the Gordian knot. But the other frequencies are also needed to bring this creativity into play. The lowest theta frequencies take you into deep meditation and have healing potential. In theta lie mystical and spiritual experiences.

Many children with attention deficit disorder (ADD) have an overabundance of theta and a deficiency of beta waves. (The antidote for such conditions is suppression of the theta and enhancement of the beta functions.)

Finally, beneath theta, we find the even slower delta waves, which operate at frequencies from 4 to 0.5 hertz (only one-half a hertz!). This is the kingdom of the inchoate unconscious, of deep sleep and restorative rest. In delta you find the desire for spirituality, inner longings, a search for meaning in life. In delta your radar is connected to intuition and psychic leaps: You think of someone and meet him on the street. You reach for the phone before it rings, and you know who is calling anyway. With delta amplified, you feel such empathy for others and have such porous boundaries that sometimes you can't tell where you begin and others leave off; and this means that you can affect the emotional state of others merely by your delta proclivities. Or conversely you can be thrown into their disrupted states, which can feel horrible until you learn to draw on the other brain-wave frequencies to maintain your boundaries. Geniuses and psychics have access to delta. Healing abilities are carried on delta as well as on theta waves.

Please note: No brain wave is better than another. They work in harmony, moving like ocean waves to form emotional or mental or spiritual states. But when you are able to access all four wavelengths *at will* and when you add the power of heightened amplification, then you *have the attributes of the Awakened Mind.*

Now you demonstrate creativity, clarity, flexibility, intuition, psychic and spiritual gifts. You know who you are. You are connected to your core, comfortable in your skin, empathic with others.

> Children up to the age of two live primarily in delta; from two to six in theta; from six to ten or even up to puberty alpha is added to the mix. The abstract thinking of beta waves comes late.

WITH THIS INTRODUCTION, George led me happily to one of his play stations. I sat in a plush black-leather reclining chair while he dabbed various places on my head with a gooey gel and placed five electrodes on me, like a crown: two in front, two on the sides, one in back. A scanner would monitor my brain waves as he gave me various problems to solve. It was interesting. Over his shoulder, I could make out the computer screen and the four horizontal stripes of color that corresponded to each frequency.

Beta—Blue
Alpha—Yellow
Theta—Green
Delta—Purple

I was first asked simply to say something while he adjusted the scanner; and choosing an incident that had recently happened to me, I told a story. My brain waves leaped into delta, as recorded by a wide stream of purple on the monitor.

He then asked me to close me eyes. "I want you to count backward from one hundred by sevens," he said. "The first is ninety-three. Please continue." Wow. This was *hard!*

I think I had reached fifty-one when he stopped me and asked me now to start a light breathing meditation. I've been meditating for years and can easily become a shell of air, filled with whiteness or pleasing light. At this point he put on soft, unmelodic New Age music, and I may have fallen asleep for a few seconds. I woke up, startled by his voice asking me to concentrate on the color red, to see the color behind my closed eyes. To my surprise, the scarlet hue appeared, flowing forth: no problem seeing red. He ran me through a medley of colors: orange, yellow, green, blue, purple. Sometimes he added other senses, like the smell of new-mown grass, for example, as I called up green, or the taste of blueberries when thinking of blue. I was surprised at how perfectly these sensations occurred. I could smell the grass and taste the oranges or blueberries on my tongue. I marveled at it. Do the senses reside inside the mind?

> *We don't understand how our psychic forces draw and replenish themselves from this [spiritual] source. . . . We're only beginning to be aware of the intuitional forces.*
>
> AMBROSE WORRALL, healer and
> aeronautical engineer

Finally, George asked me to imagine the life that I would like to have (this felt *terrific!*), and then, almost before I was ready, he started slowly bringing me back into my body, back into the room with its banks of electronics, back into the leather chair, and I was laughing with pleasure at my "trip."

Most notable healers operate in the Awakened Mind pattern (combining all four brain-wave frequencies). Merely
by remaining in the presence of a healer, the patient will
evidence a change in brain wave patterns.

"I think we're moving into a paradigm shift," Pierson said.
"With training, *everyone* can move into these altered states and
learn to use all four brain-wave frequencies. And when we do,
we enter new states of awareness and understanding. For most
people, the problem is simply to reduce the beta-wave functions
enough to slip into slower brain waves, or rather to draw up the
alpha, theta, and delta that permit the intuitive *Aha!*"

"And you can teach someone that?"

"Yes."

"Anyone?"

"Yes. We have thirty years of experience behind us."

ANTONIO, an acupuncturist and archaeologist, is also an athlete.
One day he was hiking in the high-altitude mountains above
Taos, absorbed in the sun-dappled trail, the pull of the hill on his
thighs, the towering trees, and sharp air. He was playing on a tiny
flute as he climbed, when suddenly he stopped short. He was in
an aspen grove of tall shimmering trees. A thought came to him:
It happened here. He grew very still. He stepped off the trail into
the thick green grass beneath the trees. His companions were far
behind. He was alone. His eyes searched the ground, the grass,
and then he thought, *Here.* He bent down, and at his feet picked
up a small stone. Only an archaeologist would have recognized
it. It was an arrowhead dating from 2000 BC.

He turned it in his hands, listening. What had happened that day? An Indian had shot and lost an arrow. What had he shot at? Another man? A bear? A deer? Antonio pocketed the arrowhead and walked on, wondering what intuition led him to that knowing, *It happened here.*

IT IS IN DELTA and theta that you pierce the misty boundaries into the spiritual realms. You see spirits. You commune with angels. You are psychic now; you can see into the future, work with Fate. You have only to wish, and often the dream is yours. You know how to touch the fabled Buddhist "Wish-Fulfilling Tree" of meditation, no longer a metaphor but reality. *You consciously create conditions.* The irony is, of course, that by the time you reach this state, you have lost the desire to manifest selfish things or harm another. You have come to trust Providence, Intelligence, whatever we call this Mystery of God. You enter the spiritual realms in deep humility, compassion, and gratitude. Do you want to see angels? Then ask. And when your prayers and inner longings are answered, you remember your responsibility.

You notice.

You give thanks.

You pass the gifts along.

twelve

DOWSING & VIEWING

*Perhaps the only limits to the human
mind are those we believe in.*

WILLIS HARMAN, president of IONS,
1977–1997

WHEN I WAS A LITTLE GIRL, a dowser came out to my grand-mother's farm to walk the pastures looking for water, or rather for where to place a well. Everyone who grows up in the country is familiar with these so-called water witches, who have the ability to take a slender Y-shaped branch in their hands (preferably hazel, willow, or peach), stride up and down the hills, and find by the bending of the branch the best site for drilling. (A variety of rods, straight or bent, wire or plastic, are used for dowsing as well as for finding minerals, pipes, oil, and electrical and other forces.) I was about twelve at the time, and curious. I remember I took the dowser's branch and discovered I, too, had the gift—except in reverse! The branch tore the very skin off my hands as I struggled to keep it from moving. It lifted its point skyward and twisted round, slashing, whipping me in the face! I felt humiliated when the grown-ups laughed, but I had no doubt about what happened, for I'd done everything I could to prevent the stick from moving. I don't use the gift, but on those occasions when for fun

I've tried, the wand always behaves in the reckless same way: swiveling skyward and around *toward* me instead of dipping courteously toward the earth and the water lying hidden in its depths.

My daughter and her husband have a place in Massachusetts. When they wanted to drill a well, they called in a renowned dowser.

"We want to know where to drill the well," Jonathan needlessly explained.

"Whoa. Wait. Back up. How deep do you want it? No point having to drill down too far. Shall we ask for, what, up to five hundred feet?"

"That sounds good. Okay, let's go."

"Whoa. Wait a minute. You want good-quality water, right? It should be pure. How many gallons a minute? No point getting a trickle. Shall we say fifty gallons a minute?"

Jonathan laughed. "Whew! That's a lot! But all right, why not? Better more than less."

Only then did the dowser move outside to walk their land. After a time he indicated the exact spot. "Dig here."

At roughly 250 feet, they struck the purest, most delicious water you've ever tasted flowing at, you guessed it, fifty gallons a minute.

Dousers use all sorts of tools: a wire coat hanger stretched into a long thin strip can be used; or two wires bent at ninty-degree angles and one held in each hand. At a party in Brittany, I once met a French dowser, Jean Unguen, who showed me the thin, flexible, plastic twenty-seven-inch-long wand he used to find electrical or geological fault lines. He told me how a farmer once called him to find out why the sows in one sty produced fat, healthy piglets and those in the nearby sty brought forth only sickly, weak little creatures that often died. Unguen dowsed the farmyard with his wand, made his determination, and told the farmer to place a magnet. "Here. On this fence post. And don't move it."

I don't know how the farmer managed to attach the magnet to the fence, but afterward the piglets in the unhealthy sty were born as fat and frisky as anyone could wish. Something in the farm was electrically "off."

We're out of the realm of personal intuition now, but dowsing is an age-old occupation, another tool of psychic exploration. I remember laughing with Jean Unguen as he told me tale after tale of his professional work. After a bit I asked if he could help me with my house! At the time I owned a beautiful house in the fashionable Georgetown neighborhood of Washington, D.C. The only problem was it made me sick; that is, I always felt a little poorly in the house, not badly, but enough to feel low or tired, out of sorts.

"Make a floor plan of the house when you get home," Unguen said. "Do it on graph paper, exact to the centimeter, and mail it to me. I'll dowse it with my pendulum, and then we'll talk by phone."

His Breton accent was thick enough to make me hesitate at the idea of a phone conversation, but I followed his directions, mailed him a precise floor plan, exact to the centimeter, and worked out a time to talk. He said a fault line ran diagonally under the dining room, that I needed to place a magnet in the living room to balance the fault. I'd have to phone him when I was ready, and he would indicate to me long-distance the exact site for the magnet.

The first problem was how to put a magnet in the middle of the living room floor without having it kicked or sucked up by the vacuum cleaner. Fortunately we had a "mother-in-law" apartment in the basement just below. I could attach the magnet to a ceiling panel below that hid the underside of the living room floor.

I asked my French niece over to translate for me on the telephone. Then you should have seen us as we sat on the basement floor, trying to tape the magnet to the basement ceiling (the reverse side of the living room floor). We placed the ceiling panel on the floor, the magnet on the panel. Unguen, in France, directed the operation.

"Move the magnet slightly left," he directed us, holding his pendulum over the drawing I had sent him. "Down a little. Up. Over. There! Right there!"

My family thinks I'm nuts. I taped the magnet in the exact spot and guess what? Never again did I feel ill in the house!

We're far removed, it seems, from intuition and psychic studies, precognition and clairvoyance, but they are related, at least to the degree that we don't know what's going on beyond the fact that a pendant or dowsing tool offers some people the ability to "see" or "feel" or "sense," in ways we cannot understand, things that they have no right to know.

But you don't need the wand!

I have a sensitive friend, Elizabeth Paige. One day, hiking alone in Crete (for these images often come when you are alone), she found herself in an isolated little valley with the stonework remains of an abandoned farm. She stood a few moments near one of the roofless stone huts (a former springhouse?) and shuddered as she saw with movie-clip clarity a young woman in long skirts who, standing near the hut, looked up from her work and was washed by terror. She'd seen her father leading his donkey up the hillside on his way home, and a wave of panic had swept over her, knowing that once again he would assault her. Incest! Rape! She had no way to protect herself. Her loneliness. Her helplessness. Her isolation. *Blink!* The vision lasted only a second, but it was so strong that my friend could not shake it. She hurried away. She never doubted that for one moment she'd ripped the fabric of time and seen the resonance of a real event.

IT WAS THE WRITER C. M. Mayo who suggested that if I was interested in intuition I should take a class in controlled remote viewing. I had first read about remote viewing around 1979, in the Science section (I believe) of *Newsweek*. But the term had been coined earlier by physicists Harold Puthoff and Russell Targ at Stanford Research Institute and published first in *Nature*. It caught the attention of the right people, and the CIA gave the laser physicists $50,000 to conduct formal studies. It was simple. They placed a psychic in a soundproof, lead-lined, windowless Faraday room to shield him or her from external electromagnetic waves or radiation. Three "sites" were blindly chosen at random, slipped into three sealed envelopes, and given to a driver. He was told to get in the car, choose one envelope, open it, drive to that site, and look around.

Meanwhile, the psychic, comfortable in the windowless room, was already sketching the site that *had not yet been chosen*. The sketches proved remarkably accurate. One showed a child's playground, I remember, and the psychic managed even to hear the squeak of the rusty swings and the laughter of the children.

The article made a profound impression on me, but I heard nothing more for decades. It turns out the military had also been impressed and began their secret experiments in psychic spying around this time, operating out of a purportedly abandoned shack in Fort Meade, Maryland. Lyn Buchanan was one of these military "viewers," and his book *The Seventh Sense* is a jewel of information about these now declassified experiments. When the military unit closed down in 1996, at the end of the Cold War, and Buchanan left the military, he and his wife, Linda, set

up a business, Problems Solutions Innovations (did you notice
the acronym *psi?*) to help businesses grow, find lost children,
work with police, diagnose health problems, and teach people
how to do controlled remote viewing, for it is Lyn's premise that
with practice we all have these powers.

> *CRV was not created for psychics. It was created for the
> nonpsychics, for the "ungifted."*
>
> LYN BUCHANAN

Various organizations now teach remote viewing, including
the Monroe Institute in Faber, Virginia. At my friend's suggestion, though, I chose to take the basic course from Lori Williams,
Buchanan's talented student, in Amarillo, Texas. (There are many
levels to CRV, the advanced courses being taught in Alamogordo,
New Mexico, by ex–military viewer Buchanan, but Lori teaches
the introductory basic course.)

It would take too long to explain the process and be so boring
that you would wander off to a Terry Pratchett novel or some video
game, and who could blame you? Suffice it to say that on the first
day we were taught a series of ideograms or hieroglyphs that provide a language to the wordless, imagistic subconscious mind,
allowing it to shift information into our conscious minds. The
seven ideograms are: land, water, man-made (object), biological
or organic (material), space/air, motion/energy, and natural (material). Refinements are added in later courses. Controlled remote
viewing takes left- and right-brain functions into account, but it
doesn't draw on brain-wave frequencies or energy fields.

Having taken only the basic and intermediate courses, I can
only describe my experience at this somewhat primitive level of

intuitive viewing. At the end of the first day's introduction we
were ready to try.

"Choose a number between one and twenty," said Lori.

"Seventeen."

"Is that seventeen counting from the top or from the bottom
of a stack?"

"From the top."

"Good." She left the room together with Karen, my classmate, took an inch-thick file of photographs, counted seventeen
pages from the top, slipped number seventeen into a folder, and
returned.

"Okay," she said. "What is the target?"

"What! Are you crazy?"

"Work the site. You know how to do it now. Use the
ideograms."

The amazing thing is how much you know! It may take an
hour to "work" a target, or even days; the choice is left entirely up
to you.

In the advanced classes you learn to determine dimensions
(length/width/height), history, time frames, and various other
factors that permit not only viewing the target through a glass
darkly but also putting the various pieces into a cohesive whole
in order to understand the image or site itself.

CRV found that intuitive functions are highest when performed within one hour of each side of 1,347 hours sidereal (or star) time. They are lowest within half an hour of
each side of 1,800 hours. Sidereal time differs from solar
time by four minutes a day. On only one day a year are the
two the same. A sidereal clock is required for calculating
sidereal time.

THERE'S A CERTAIN IRONY to the fact that it's the military that hacked a pathway into this wilderness of intuition, and you can't help but admire the sturdy, structural discipline of the military approach. On a sheet of paper, any conscious reasoning of left-brain logic is recorded down the right-hand side of the page. The illumined intuition of right-brain insight is recorded on the left-hand side of the sheet. This is in accordance with the way the left brain governs the right side of the body, and the right brain governs the left side.

While searching with the right-brain inner eye, you occupy your analytical mind by jotting on the right-hand side of the paper every thought, conclusion, doubt, and castle it wants to build in the air. Conscious thoughts are recognizable as sentences and nouns, for the perceiving intuitive mind works only in symbols, imagery, and descriptive adjectives and adverbs. It knows no nouns. If you think "squirrel," therefore, you record it as a left-brain conscious thought. If you think "small, biological, furry, swinging, stopping, scooting, quick," you can be pretty sure you are "viewing" with right-hemisphere intuition. Remote viewing insight only describes.

One interesting phenomenon: When your subconscious mind is fully activated, perceiving, you lose the ability to spell and write. Your hand shakes. Seeing in pictures, you lose words. Instead, you draw.

Only the military could have dredged, mined, sorted, sifted, and sculpted this brilliant entry into intuition, the Seeing Soul, as it were (though the military would not call it that), whereby anybody—you, me, your little sister, your irritable husband, your defiant disbeliever, anyone at all—can work the puzzle.

Is time a barrier? No. Space? Piffle! You leap over tall buildings in a single bound, flying to far countries quick as thought. Wonder Woman and other superheroes—they all have less sophisticated skills than the ones we everyday perceivers utilize! And, most astonishing, it takes only one three-day weekend and considerable practice to hone these skills. (After the weekend, you have to practice with the discipline of a martial art, to which it is compared, for it takes practice, practice, practice to get good at it.) I don't need to add that all "remote viewers" have poor sessions sometimes, coming up blank, but often they hit the target spot on. No meditation is involved, no tarot or crystal balls, no pendulum or smoking incense, no crystals, no angels, no spirit guides—nothing but your inner wisdom as you listen to your heightened perceptions, aware of sites far distant from your senses.

I think the subconscious, if it is indeed the seat of intuition, is usually consigned to the basement, chained like a madman in the cellar from whence his howls and banshee wails cause shivers in the upstairs host ("Quick! Pour another drink!"). Demonic, we call it, or the work of the devil, without understanding that the luminous and inarticulate presence of this voice of glory is always on our side.

THOSE ASSOCIATED with Buchanan's controlled remote viewing are careful to assert that this acquired skill is *different from psychic abilities!* Nonetheless, they claim it increases intuition, as the subconscious learns a way of communicating with the conscious mind.

"The difference," wrote Lyn Buchanan to me in an e-mail, "is actually a very large one, in that intuition or psychic faculties is an ability. CRV is a set of tools that give you control over the ability." The tools are based, he continued, on discipline and practice, on mind-brain studies, and on interviewing or reporting techniques.

If psychic gifts are likened to a vacation in the country, controlled remote viewing is the car that takes you there quickly and under your own power. Once you are at the vacation site, it gives you freedom and mobility. The car is not the vacation, but it's an efficient mechanism for controlling your trip. And then he added, distinguishing his work perhaps from that of some others, "Remote viewing is the New Age term for 'psychic ability.' *Controlled* remote viewing is the name of the set of tools that put you in control while you're using your gifts."

CRV is not a toy. It can be dangerous. I spoke earlier of the blurring of boundaries, especially in children. With controlled remote viewing you may get sucked into the target in the same way, caught in a mud slide, or blown up by a bomb; or, if it is a human, you can enter so fully into the mental state of the subject that his way of thinking becomes yours, at least for the duration of the session—a danger if you're viewing a psychopath.

"Mental access," writes Buchanan, "at the level provided by the CRV process can be very dangerous to the viewer." When the target is a person, you *describe*; you don't try to access or get inside the other person's mind! The boundaries are slippery, enchanted, and entrancing, as you will see in the following chapters.

Inviting Intuition IV:
Using the Pendulum

Because everyone is different, there are no hard-and-fast rules for learning intuition, except the one concerning stillness and deep listening. But once you can easily attain a quiet and attentive "no-mind" state, the pendulum becomes a wondrous tool.

You may use any pendant hanging on a chain or string. A sewing needle works perfectly. Thread the needle with about twelve inches of thread and tie a knot (to keep it on the needle). Hold the knot, allowing the needle to swing free. (It may be easier to see if you hold it over a dark surface or your hand.)

Empty your mind. Go into the space of no-mind.

First you must create a relationship between yourself and your pendulum. Ask the needle to show you "Yes." When I do it, the "Yes" presents as a vertical swing or, sometimes, when the pendulum is wildly enthusiastic, as high, fast, *clock wise* circles.

For "No," the pendulum swings horizontally back and forth or else in passionate counterclockwise sweeps. But bear in mind that if your pendulum reverses this signal, that's perfectly all right! What's important is that you and your pendulum work together and that you both understand the signature.

Once you feel comfortable with your pendulum, you begin to work with it. Remember it can respond only with Yes or No. Your questions, therefore, must be phrased in such a way that it can provide you with either a positive or negative answer. If you ask something like "What shall I do about X?" the pendulum, helpless, will either stand still or weave the air in sinuous coils, expressing hesitation, anguish, frustration, like a dragon coiled in its lair. Break the question down.

"Should I contact X?"

"Yes."

"By e-mail?"

"No."

"By phone?"

"Yes."

"Should I phone tomorrow?"

"Yes."

"Should I call before twelve noon? Before ten o'clock? Between ten-thirty and eleven o'clock?"

"Should I apologize?"

By the time you use your pendulum daily or even several times a day, you will have acquired one that appeals to you—a jeweled watch fob, perhaps, a gold cross, or an amethyst carved and shaped into a fine point—and you'll ask your questions and receive responses swift as thought: no one could imagine what you've done. But until that time and while you are learning, I suggest that each time you pick up your pendulum, you ask it for permission to work with you. Each time ask it to show you Yes and No. (There's no point misreading the message from your higher senses).

Each time ask it three questions: *Could* I ask you about X? *Should* I ask about X? And finally, *May* I ask?

If you receive a deliberate "Yes" for each of the three, then boldly form your questions. You can also use the pendulum for long-sighted, farsighted information.

Your questions may be as important as whether to quit your job or change your daughter's school. Or they may be as silly as whether your husband, who is traveling, is still asleep or if he can be phoned. Let's say you've planned to meet a friend in a café and you forgot to confirm. Will he be there? Ask your pendulum. It will tell you. (You could also call on your cell phone, I agree.)

I used to dislike pendulum dowsing simply because I could make the pendant give any answer that I chose! But once you learn to empty yourself of desire for an outcome the pendulum becomes another useful tool.

The Ethics of Dowsing

Never use your pendulum in a public space, like a subway or business meeting, where strangers can see you. (Of course, if you are participating in a psychic circle or using it to give a reading on behalf of someone else, that's another story.)

There are several reasons. First, someone may be tempted maliciously to deflect it by sending it a contradictory thought (psychokinesis), and don't imagine that the pendulum won't respond. Or, someone could unconsciously interfere merely by the strength of his or her energy field, and torque your answer like a compass needle shifted from true north.

But second, it's not respectful of either the pendulum or the people around you.

Keep your pendulum in a pure and private place. Treasure it.

Remember that the pendulum, like a crystal ball or the tarot, is nothing but a tool. As you become adept, you may set it aside. You'll scry with your perfected intuition. The answer comes instantly without the tool. Even then, however, if you've been ill or thrown off center by an unexpected blow, you may wish to revert to the pendulum. If you haven't used it in a while, remember to begin each time afresh, asking it for Yes and No.

Part III

ENCHANTED BOUNDARIES

*It no longer seems possible to brush aside
the study of so-called occult facts.*

SIGMUND FREUD

thirteen

SPEAKING OF SPIRITS

Is there another Life? Shall I awake and find all this a dream? There must be. We cannot be created for this sort of suffering.

JOHN KEATS, in a letter

MANY YEARS AGO, Annabel Stehli, a friend of mine, phoned to say she had a tape she wanted me to listen to.

We were living in Brooklyn Heights at the time, and Annabel, a single woman with two little girls, lived a few streets over. Dotsie developed leukemia at age four, and Georgiana, the younger child, was autistic. The father had run out. (*Of course!* I thought indignantly on behalf of my lovely friend. *Just like a man!*) They lived in a small upstairs apartment overlooking a noisy street, and Annabel was in danger of unraveling. Two babies, both with disabilities, and sweet though they were, it was hard for her to make it through a day. Dotsie's hair had fallen out from the chemotherapy, and her joints and face were swollen. She was young and innocent, and she was sick, poor little thing. She hurt, and the fact that her younger sister could not speak, could not look you in the face, could not play with other children, including mine, when we came over for a playdate or to help out Annabel— all combined to make it hard for Annabel.

At age eight, Dotsie died. A year or more passed, and one day

Annabel phoned me. She had just returned from England, she said, where she'd seen the famous medium Ena Twigg.

"What's a medium?" I asked in my simplicity.

"I have a tape." She was bursting with excitement. "Will you listen to it? I want you to tell me what you think."

She came over to my apartment. We put the tape into the recorder, and soon the voice of the medium with her English accent filled the room. A moment later her voice changed, and a chill ran down me. It was Dotsie! I knew that voice. I knew that child! There was no doubt in my mind. Moreover, as if to dispel any questions her mother might have had, the voice of Dotsie told how one day after she had died she had watched her mother weeping while folding up her little clothes. Then she described a moment, a single act that no one but her mother could have known.

"It's true!" said Annabel, her face alight. "It's true!"*

That was the first time I heard about mediumship. Never did I imagine that I would acquire intuitive gifts myself (though nothing approaching the level of the magnificent Ena Twigg) and never did I realize that we all have it within our power to cross these boundaries. Some people are more naturally gifted than others, but I'm convinced we all can do it!

But before I was able to understand these things, years of learning lay ahead of me. First I had to accept the possibility that there was indeed a spiritual dimension (or more than one), that the soul lives on after death, that angels and spirits may be more than metaphor, and that we are all subject to moments of

---

* There's more to the story. It has a happy end. Years later, when Georgie was around eleven, her mother and stepfather found an audiologist in Switzerland who, in twenty half-hour sessions over a period of ten days, completely healed Georgie of both her dyslexia and the hyperacute hearing disorder that, diagnosed from birth as autism, had kept her in institutions for years. The story is beautifully told in *The Sound of a Miracle* by Annabel Stehli (New York: Beaufort Books, 1995).

grace, inexplicably enfolding us in love. And this, despite the fact (am I particularly dense?) that I had been reared in the Episcopal Church, after all, which taught belief in God and the afterlife, in the love and forgiveness of a Holy Spirit. Somehow I needed proof before I could accept the teachings as true. Yet evidence abounded. It was all around me. As long ago as 1758, the mystic Swedenborg had visited Queen Louisa Ulrika of Sweden, who asked him to tell her something about her deceased brother Augustus William. The next day, Swedenborg whispered something in her ear. Turning pale, she explained that what she'd heard was something only she and her brother could know. Another time a woman who had lost an important document came to the famous clairvoyant, asking if a recently deceased person could tell him where it was, and this information, too, he passed along.

WHEN I WAS A CHILD, I was afraid of the dark. We lived in the Maryland countryside. Today the landscape is covered by developments, but in those days when no one lived nearby, the tall oaks towered over the roof, swaying gently like sea kelp and casting a greenish light over us, as if we lived underwater. But at night the darkness was immense. We never went outside at night.

In summer, of course, the long, slow, pearl dusk lit by fireflies kept the night at bay until we children were well in bed. But in winter the family crouched in the small study, our parents and we three kids, until our mother would nod to me.

"Time for bed. Give a kiss good night."

I dreaded bedtime. My parents didn't think to walk me upstairs, and I knew better than to invite their ridicule, ask for coddling.

"She's afraid of the dark!" They would have laughed and then, impatient: "Now, go on. There's nothing there."

From the small study I had to cross the pitch-black down-stairs hall. It took all my courage to leap into the pit toward the light switch on the far wall, right next (oh, horror!) to the yawn-ing black doorway of the formal living room. Once there, safe for a moment in a yellow pool of the light, I stood helpless, staring into the black hole up the stairs.

I could turn on the light from downstairs and climb the lit stairwell, but even so, once upstairs I had to flick off the light at the far wall and dash through darkness—five steps—to my room! (No one thought of leaving lights on, and the possibility never entered my head, so trained were we to save electricity.)

Why was I so afraid? The grown-ups walked through the black rooms without a thought, familiar as they were with the numb stability of chairs and tables. But to me the dark was filled with subtle movement, a shifting of air, a kind of silent breathing, and a sense of being watched.

Things . . . watching.

Later, when I was grown and living in other rooms in other houses, I'd sometimes catch the flicker of a shadow at the corner of my eye and turn to see . . . nothing there. Sometimes I'd shud-der at the uncomfortable sensation that someone was in the room with me. I'd swivel around, only to find the room empty. Was it my imagination? The play of light? My eyesight was excel-lent; these instincts weren't the consequence of impaired vision. Yet this—what do I call it?—*enhanced acuity* of the senses car-ried over into adulthood.

Spirits are usually seen with peripheral vision, out of the corner of your eyes. A flash and they are gone. They are sensed with the "spiritual eye."

I didn't believe in ghosts or spirits. For that matter I didn't even believe in God (at least not as the white-bearded, erratic, male, Old Testament deity I'd read about, and I wasn't so sure of the Father that Jesus offered either, no one having told me that our images of God might grow and change as we mature). Yet I believed in Something that I didn't understand. I'd stand speechless sometimes at the beauty of a tree, a pond, the bravery of a squirrel. And sometimes shiver as if touched by the trailing of a will-o'-the-wisp.

I'm telling you all this as an introduction to my fear of dying. (This was before I met my first ghost or had my life saved by an angel or experienced most of the events that awakened my consciousness.)

I was twenty-four or -five. It had only recently dawned on me that I could be extinguished utterly, and at night I lay in bed beside my husband, rigid with terror, my thoughts flying and fleeing this apprehension of reality, scrabbling for escape. Of course, I'd known about death since the age of two: The cat had died. So, too, the chickens, mice, goldfish, dogs. But they weren't *me*, and I suppose you have to reach a certain level of maturity before you can grasp that egocentric fact. In teen age, you're impregnable, immortal, immutable, a god.

So there I was at twenty-five, lying in the dark in bed, thinking about being dead, and, worse, seeing no way out and knowing that my own death was coming closer with every passing day (time hauling me handcuffed toward the Infinite Dark). Finally I decided that contemplating my extinction, as I was doing, was driving me insane. Was I clinging to an egoistic, isolated notion of a *self*? One night, defeated, I gave up, decided to think about it no more, excepting the desperate, inarticulate, and silent prayer "Save me, God!" (At the time I had no concept of the Buddhist doctrine of *anatman*, the theory of "no-self" or "no-soul,"

just as I knew nothing of the Buddhist "emptiness" of all phenomena or understood the Wisdom Books of Ecclesiastes, be-
moaning that all is emptiness, all vanity.)

> *There is but one freedom, to put oneself right with death.*
> *After that, everything is possible. . . . Believing in God*
> *amounts to coming to terms with death. When you have*
> *accepted death, the problem of God will be solved—and*
> *not the reverse.*
>
> ALBERT CAMUS

Years passed. I had children. Gradually, caught in the busy-
ness of living, I forgot about dying.

And then my mother died. We'd had a stormy relationship, as
I struggled for independence and she to impress on me some sem-
blance of respectability. She was an intuitive herself, prescient,
emotional. I see her still, the way she dragged the little tractor
around the patchy two-acre lawn. She would stop to rest and look
out over the valley to the line of trees that marked a stream below.
She drew energy from the earth, the view, the towering trees. My
mother "knew" things.

Once she dreamed of shipwrecked people on a raft, rising
and gliding down the slopes of high waves. In the dream she saw
the coordinates for the raft. The next morning she heard on the
radio that a plane had crashed in the Pacific. She was aghast, but
what could she do? Whom could she telephone to tell of such a
dream, and who would believe her if she tried?

Cassandra, daughter of Priam in the *Iliad*, had visions, foresight, dreams. She prophesied the fall of Troy and to her horror
foresaw the city set aflame, herself enslaved and carried to a foreign

land. She was made mad by the slaughter, rape, and butchery she forecast; made mad by virtue of her intuition, her gifts of precognition and prophecy, that showed what anguish lay in store: mad with horror, mad with grief, mad with the loneliness and isolation of farsighted intuition. She could not tell, and others could not hear.

It is no accident that the Greek seer Tiresias was blind—the perfect metaphor for insight. Or that the prophecies of the Delphic Oracle came from the dark cavern in the rocks from whence arose the smoky steaming breath of the earth and gods.

One-half of all spontaneous *psi* experiences occur in dreams. Many involve the death of a family member or loved one.

INTUITION THAT COMES in the form of a dream is as old as folklore itself. Plutarch reports how Calpurnia, wife of Julius Caesar, dreamed of the danger to her husband on March 15, the ides of March. She begged him to stay home that fateful morning and not walk down to the Roman Forum to attend the Senate. He refused her admonitions and premonitions and thus was stabbed by the Roman senators, who feared he'd end the Republic by naming himself dictator.

For naught. His nephew Augustus grabbed power during the ensuing civil war, crowned himself emperor, and finished off the Republic anyway.

There are some who say that our dreams are given us by angels, spirit guides. And others that our subconscious mind, unable to make itself heard above the clatter of the conscious mind, forces its intuitions on us as imagery in the form of dreams.

Word associations immediately after awakening from a
dream are 29 percent more likely to be unusual than those
later in the day.

BACK TO MY MOTHER. One day she died. And my own views
of the afterlife changed.

After her death, she made her presence known insistently,
and usually with her own quirky sense of humor. The first instance, perhaps a few days after the funeral, occurred when my
sister and brother and I were looking for a particular document.
We couldn't find it anywhere. Finally, we stood in the pantry
looking at one another helplessly.

"Where could it possibly be?"

"I know!" my brother cried, and he dashed down the basement steps.

A moment later he returned with the legal document in his
hand. "It was in a file cabinet at the back of the cellar."

"How in the world did you know where to look?"

He looked at us in bafflement. "I didn't even know there was
a file cabinet there."

Intuition? Clairvoyance? We laughed. We knew our mother's
work: thoughts inserted in his head.

The second one took place months later. After my mother
died I used to drive to Baltimore from Washington once or twice
a week to see my father, who had suffered a stroke. He was fortunate to have nurses caring for him. He didn't have to go into
assisted living. But his life was sad and lonely without his wife of
fifty years. The house felt quiet now without her busy footsteps
clattering across the wooden floors. Yet oddly, I never opened the
front door without feeling the welcome of her presence, as if she

were still hanging around. Waiting for Daddy. "My imagination," I thought, and reproved myself for wishful thinking.

Sometimes I brought along my daughter, then twelve, and because I wanted her to have fond memories of these visits to her grandfather, I found some horses nearby for us to ride. We would visit Daddy, go off to ride for an hour, come back to have tea and talk with him. I would do the talking, holding his limp hand, telling him the news and loving him while he listened, eyes shining or sometimes dulled with the exhausted despair of those imprisoned by a stroke. I had the helpless feeling that these visits were never enough. I couldn't help him.

One day we came in the house, sat with my father for a while, and then left for our ride. When we returned, Bernice, the nurse, announced, "There's no water in the house."

"What do you mean?"

"It happened right after you left. We had water then. Remember, you had a cup of tea? When you left, I went to the kitchen to make lunch, and all of a sudden the spigots spit out air. The toilets don't flush. It happened right after you two left."

"We need a plumber."

But first I went down to the gloomy basement to investigate. There, in a cavern off to one side, a pump sucked up well water with heaving gasps that used to thrill and terrify us as children. The pump room was the heartbeat of the house, and only my mother knew how it worked. I took a flashlight and clumped down the narrow basement steps and back to the dank Etruscan cave, sweeping the light around the dark cinder-block walls, unsure of what I'd be looking for anyway. To my surprise, the floor was ankle-deep in water.

I shone the flashlight around, and there in the far corner, behind the pump, I saw an open faucet, only inches from the ground, with water pouring out.

I took off my shoes and socks, waded through the pond, and turned the spigot off.

"It's on!" came a cry from the kitchen overhead. "The water's back on."

"Oh, Mummy!" I burst out laughing! Only my mother knew there even *was* a faucet there, and my heart rejoiced as I put my shoes back on. She was still in the house, playing jokes on us. Telling us that she was still around.

But how could a spirit turn a spigot on? That takes physical force. Do we conclude either that the faucet turned itself on (this once, and never before or since) or that spirits can actually move a physical weight? I read somewhere that a spirit can move three pounds. When the son of a man I know died, the grieving father found his son's baseball cap mysteriously shifting around the house—the top of the bookcase, his computer, the boy's old room, his own.

I'm told that spirits have a special relationship to water. I had a great friend, Dorothy Clarke, then well into her nineties. Her daughter had tragically died by falling off a balcony, and soon after Jane's death her mother found that each time she took her broom out of the closet, water poured out of the straw onto the floor. It's important to note that Dorothy always set the broom upside down in the closet, handle to the floor, having learned as a child that this is the proper way to conserve the straw. Now, each time she pulled out the broom, a cup or two of water poured onto the kitchen floor. There was no leak in the closet, not even a water pipe nearby. One day she announced to me, "I keep thinking it must be Jane doing this. Do you think Jane could be sending me a message?"

After this, the broom stopped filling with water, which was as curious as the fact that it had overflowed so copiously during the previous weeks. Had Jane's spirit wanted only to be acknowledged? Was she sending a message of the water of new life?

The Sunday after her father died, a friend, grieving, stayed home from Mass while her mother and sister attended. "I just have a feeling," she said. "An intuition. I don't know why, but I think I should stay home." She didn't believe in an afterlife; yet what she wanted more than anything was to know that her father was somehow all right.

When the two women returned from church, she met them, beaming. "You won't guess what happened!" Their uncle had phoned from Hawaii to say that he'd had a curious dream the night before, in which his dead brother told him he had to phone home and tell his daughters that their father was all right, that everything was fine.

You hear story after story like this. You'd think this matter of angels and apparitions would be out of order in this work on intuition, but no. If consciousness continues after death, is it too difficult to believe that those who loved us on earth would not still be guiding, protecting, guarding us? And could they do so any better than by popping thoughts into our mind? Is it too far-fetched to think that intuition may be associated with attending spirits?

I used to wonder if all intuitions were not angels at work. I've come to believe, however, that we have these gifts within ourselves. We are souls incarnated into physical bodies, and we come trailing clouds of glory from the other world (or worlds). We come with all the manifestations and abilities of divinity. The trick is to hear with the heart, for intuitions come not from intellect but from an opening, a loosening of inhibitions, an awareness of our connection to one another and to all sentient life. It requires deep listening and a compassionate heart energy, if I may use so imprecise a term. It is our right as spiritual beings. The information is carried on spiritual energy waves and received at the core of our souls, and if angels are also involved, I say, well and good.

I've had many experiences with spirits now, and they are different from anything I might have imagined as a child, not the least of which is your curious lack of fear. It's quite unlike the depictions in movies, where the spirits leap screaming from a closet and scare the bejesus out of you. Or like the ghost of Hamlet's father, who disappears at first cock's crow. In real life (or afterlife) they hover around all day, and they seem not only kindly and helpful but terribly anxious to communicate. They are happy, young, in perfect health. They love us deeply, and they are fascinated by our world.

SPIRITS LIKE TECHNOLOGY. Again and again we hear of lights flickering, or the TV turning off and on. Or the record player going on all by itself, playing the favorite song of your brother, who just died. In one story, the grieving girlfriend alone in her apartment fell asleep listening to one record and woke up to her boyfriend's favorite song, which was on the reverse of the record. (How could the record have turned itself over?) Sometimes others will "feel" the presence of the spirit when they meet you, confirming your own sense of him still hanging around, but eventually the spirit must leave. There's work to be done; there's some "place" or dimension it's supposed to be.

Ted Greene, my anthropologist friend, says that when he was around forty, he renewed a friendship with his best friend from high school. He had not seen Wayne in years and found, as happens with some friendships, that they picked up with the same intimacy and delight they had shared years earlier.

And then Wayne got cancer. They talked about his dying. Ted asked Wayne to come after he died and tell him about it. Ted visited him in the hospital just before flying on a mission to Santo Domingo, and as he left his friend's room, walking down the hospital corridor, he had a premonition that he would never see

Wayne again. He broke into tears. A few days later, Wayne's wife phoned him in Santo Domingo with the word that his friend had died.

That night as Ted lay reading in bed, Wayne suddenly materialized. Ted freaked. Immediately the image vanished. Ted groped his way to the kitchen for a glass of water and regained control.

"Why would I be afraid of Wayne?" he asked himself, and then forced himself to lie down again, relax, and see if his friend would return.

"Relax, relax," he admonished himself. "I accept. I want him to come."

At this point Wayne reappeared.

"I'm not supposed to be here." He spoke telepathically. "I'm breaking a big rule. But we always made a point of breaking rules, didn't we?" The spirit laughed. "I can't stay. There's someplace I'm supposed to be." The important news for Ted, however, was that he was happy. Things were good. Death brings no extinguishment; we live on afterward.

Ted has no interest in developing his gift, if a gift it is, but as an anthropologist he's aware that all the so-called primitive cultures lay claims to these mysterious powers. He believes they are our natural heritage, wiped out of Westerners by the speed and hurry of our technological lives.

In psychology, physiology and medicine, whenever a debate between the mystics and the scientists has been . . . decided, it is the mystics who have usually proved to be right about the facts, while the scientists had the better of it in respect to theories.

WILLIAM JAMES

SPIRITS COME BACK in many forms, especially in dreams, but they seem to have a special affinity for birds or butterflies, winged elements. I heard of one woman who loved robins. Soon after her death, her daughter was in her kitchen, when suddenly a robin landed on the windowsill and began to peck at the glass. It wouldn't stop! It pecked and pecked. The daughter approached the window, held up her hand, and still the bird did not fly off.

"Mother, is that you?" The robin stopped pecking, hopped on the sill, peered at her with one cocked black eye, pecked one last time, and flew away. She burst into tears.

A man driving down the road thinking of the father he had lost found his car suddenly surrounded by a swarm of yellow butterflies. "My dad," he thought, for if there was anything his father had loved, it was butterflies.

I recently heard of a man whose black Lab was stricken with prostate cancer. One night he saw an owl perched in the branches of the tree outside his bedroom window—an owl he had never seen before and never saw again. A day or two later, the dog died, and he remembered the Native American belief that an owl will come to help a soul move to the Other Side.

How odd that these apparitions seem to come "suddenly." They don't last long—a greeting, an appearance in some physical form—and almost as swiftly they have gone.

Soon after my cousin died, his wife and daughter saw a magnificent antlered stag cross the lawn of their suburban Maryland home, stalk up to the picture window, and stare in at them, then turn to step majestically to the grieving widow's favorite bush, drop his head, and snatch a bite. He gazed at them from huge dark eyes and moved serenely into the woods. The two women watched in astonishment, certain that this was no normal stag.

And this is one of the marks of these engagements with animals, dreams, or intuitions: that the percipients can't shake the idea that the events are beyond the ordinary.

Patricia Kratzer is an unwilling clairsentient who works as director of finance at Imagination Stage, the children's theater, near Washington, D.C. She is English by birth, and most of her experiences have taken place in Europe.

"It only happens with people whom I trust, in a healing class, for instance, when people are holding hands. Suddenly a spirit will appear." Patricia doesn't *see* people, but she hears and feels them. In these moments she can't breathe. Often tears spring to her eyes. It's easy, she says, to categorize these "comings" as products of her imagination. Her mother, however, can tell when a spirit has come to her, for Patricia's clairsentience has gone on since childhood.

"Relax," her mother will say. "Ask, 'What do you want to tell me?'"

Patricia is not altogether comfortable with her gift. If she's aware of a little elf running back and forth, she's left wondering, What is it? What is real? At one time she thought to cut out: "It's not something I want entering me."

"Entering you?" I asked in our interview. Her choice of words intrigued me.

"I don't see them. They're inside me. I hear them talking. I can't go past the Vietnam Memorial," she continued. "I hear the screams."

Once, while staying at an ancient inn in Cornwall with her diplomat husband (himself an atheist), "I saw horrible things. I woke up. There were people everywhere, some grabbing at me. Some wore the eighteenth-century costumes of highwaymen. Later I learned they used to hang the highwaymen right there at the site of the inn."

Christy Vinson is another spirit magnet. Skinny and nervous, she talks fast and a lot. She has attracted spirits since early childhood, having acquired the gift through both her mother and grandmother, but only recently has it intruded into her life.

Seeing spirits hasn't been easy for her.

"I wish I could say it's been a fluffy, love-filled experience, that I've sailed along the last six years or so on calm waters of peace and grace, but it has not been smooth at all. I don't talk about it around the PTA or our marketing business, or friends and neighbors. They know the 'old me.' I'm the same me, except now I see and feel beings from the Other Side." She calls them passed ones.

The apparitions often appear in her bedroom as she is going to sleep, or they awaken her in the night—passed ones of all ages and appearances. She will get a "hit" of death by car accident, or by cancer, or by heart attack. At first she was afraid, not knowing what to do or how to help.

"You see, it's not just that they show up and freak me out by looking creepy. It seems to be first a way of letting me know 'how' they passed and then an indication of their present 'condition': afraid or sad, or angry, lost, unhappy, whatever."

One night a soldier appeared at the foot of her bed, glaring at her. He stayed . . . and stayed.

"You have to go! This is my home! Go away! I need to sleep!"

For four hours she prayed for the soldier, convinced he needed to move on, get out, go to the Other Side. She asked Jesus ("since He was human and must understand us humans and our difficulties") and also the soldier's guardian angel to help.

"Suddenly, to my alarm and amazement, into the bedroom came a whirlpool of light about the size of a doorway, complete with sparkles and rainbow colors. It flew up to the ceiling, and I could see a woman reaching out her arms to him (perhaps a mom or grandma) along with several tall, angelic figures. He was almost sucked into the light and disappeared."

Relieved, she fell asleep.

SOON AFTER THE SUDDEN DEATH of her husband of thirty-one years, JoAnne Zawitoski had a dream. She never saw her husband, but in her dream a voice asked if she would accept finding her husband's missing class ring and his pocket PC as a sign that her husband was well and happy, still alive with consciousness. She said yes, for both items had been missing since his death.

That morning her son found the ring tucked deep into the seat of his father's car (why would he have taken it off there?), and two days later her husband's boss phoned to say the pocket PC had been found at his office—did she want it back?

Even though JoAnne had agreed in the dream that she would "believe" if the two items were found, she didn't feel comforted. She wanted *him* back.

Of course, not everyone believes in a spirit world. One friend of mine was at my house for dinner soon after his mother died. Curious (and with my usual tactlessness), I asked, "Have you seen her since she died?"

"What do you mean?" He was taken aback.

"I mean, has she come back to tell you she's all right?"

"Of course not."

We were silent a moment. "Except last night," he added, "I had the most vivid dream about her. It was so real. She was standing by the bed. She was happy. Is that what you mean? But nothing *happened*."

fourteen

SENSITIVES & PSYCHICS

[Man] . . . is a microcosm, or a little
world, because he is an extract from all
the stars and planets of the whole
firmament, from the earth and the
elements, and so he is their quintessence.

PARACELSUS

I USED TO LAUGH at psychics and palmists, tarot and tea-leaf readers. I looked down on the charlatan with her neon sign ("Miss Sophie's Psychic Readings: $5.00"). Fraud! Superstition! Smoke and mirrors. Nonetheless I remember once visiting a seer with my sister on a lark. We were only young girls. We came into her Gypsy tabernacle, bemused by the multipatterned curtains swaying from the ceiling and walls, and the little, round, cloth-covered table boasting its crystal ball. It had all the trappings of a movie set.

I don't remember anything about the reading except being startled by the Gypsy's perceptions. She was a psychic, not a medium, and there were no frightening gestures or invitations to spirits to contact us.

A psychic uses intuition—sheer knowing; a medium, mediating between two worlds, accesses spirits or channels guides.

She told me I'd marry a man named David, a prediction I laughed off, since at the time I knew twelve men with that name. (The fact that I later married a David did, however, screw her prediction into my brain.) Afterward, my sister and I, buckling with laughter, fell back out onto the street. How had she done it? Did she have mirrors? Had she overheard us talking before she joined us in her inner sanctum?

Another time I had my palm read at a New Jersey County Fair together with my best friend, Corinne. Corinne had slipped off her engagement ring to fool the palmist, for though we were willing to plunk down our money, we certainly didn't "believe" in this stuff; we were young girls having fun. Again, the psychic was decked out in turban and Gypsy robes. She told my friend that she would not marry for three years, and this time, too, we left her tent bursting with laughter, because her wedding was scheduled in only a few months. As it happened, Corinne broke the engagement and didn't marry for several more years.

After that I had nothing more to do with psychics. I was busy raising my children, worrying about my marriage, my father's stroke, my mother's cancer, and just the demands of making a living.

Fast-forward several decades. I was in the middle of a divorce, separated from my husband and children, confused, and groping. A friend urged me to see the Reverend F. Reed Brown, a psychic, at the Arlington Metaphysical Chapel in the Virginia suburbs. I was unhappy enough to agree. Later, I became friends with Reed and even took some classes with him, but at the time I was simply knocked off my pins by his insight. I assumed it was somehow a fix.

The Arlington Metaphysical Chapel is a pretty little white clapboard building with lovely stained-glass windows. It has that special musty scent of hymnals and flowers, a place of quiet prayer. Reed's office was a small room off the entranceway. He was reading for someone else when I arrived, for that was what he did: see people, hour after hour. I prayed in the church until I was called into his tiny cluttered office.

On arrival, I'd been instructed to write down the names of three people who had passed over and all my questions on the same three-by-five-inch card, fold the card in half, and then in half again, until it made a tiny wad. Brown stood up behind his desk as I entered. He was a roly-poly man in his middle age, with a cheerful smile and an open, cordial hand. A man delighted to live in his own skin. On the wall behind him hung a portrait of a white-bearded man. I learned later that it was Dr. Peebles, his special familiar, or spirit guide.

Reed slapped a tape into his tape recorder for me. He took my card and asked me to cover his hand with mine, said a prayer for guidance, then dropped the card (I picked it up), sat back, and proceeded to tell me the three names on the card and to answer all my questions.

I was stunned. How had he done that? Were there cameras in the entrance hall? Even so, no camera could have read the card; my handwriting is smaller than the footprints of fairies. I can hardly read it myself! One especially interesting moment struck me. One of my questions concerned a friend of mine named Page. Reed leaned back in his chair, one hand to his forehead. He tapped the third eye. "I'm seeing a book, a beautiful book, and pages are turning. They are fine pages, covered with writing, and they are turning one by one. One by one. Does this mean anything to you?"

"No," I said, baffled.

"No matter. What I'm getting is that you aren't to make any

moves. This is all being orchestrated by Above. You're not to worry. Everything will turn out the way it's supposed to."

It was only as I was driving home that I remembered I'd asked about my friend Page! Dope! I'd totally forgotten my question by the middle of the reading. (For one thing, I was still puzzling out how in the world he had managed to tell me the first names of my mother and father, who, he said, were watching over me proudly from the Other Side.)

I found the reading interesting but did not go back for years. One day my friend Ted Greene, the Harvard anthropologist who was working then with the State Department, asked if I wanted to go with him while he consulted Anne Gehman, a well-known medium in Virginia. (This is the same Ted who years later told me about seeing the spirit of his friend Wayne after his death.)

"A *medium*!? *You're going to a medium?*" I burst out laughing. But I was also curious. After all, Ted is an intellectual; I wanted to know what in the world he thought he was doing.

Driving there, Ted told me how, in an earlier reading, Anne Gehman had informed him that his mother was sick and that the family should pay attention. When he'd forced his mother to see a doctor, they found she had Parkinson's disease.

"Oh."

We went to a well-kept suburban office similar to a doctor's office. Anne was a pleasant woman a little younger than me, and I was surprised at how down-to-earth and ordinary she appeared, and how much I liked her. (It was the same with Brown: how professional and high-spirited and how *ordinary* he was—and how anything but.) While she gave Ted his reading, I waited in the comfortable, well-appointed anteroom and leafed through the magazines in the basket, none of which were on psychic matters, feeling a little envious that I wasn't getting a reading, too.

As we drove away, Ted told me what she said. I was impressed. This medium was quite different from the psychic of my imagination who bends over your palm while intoning, "You are very sensitive, you've been unhappy, no one understands you," and charges fifty dollars for words that could apply to anyone.

But I was still far from the realization that we all have these abilities or that they can be developed. I didn't know that the more you love, the more psychic and intuitive you become. I didn't know that, made fearless by the ardor of your love, you dare to trust the Universe—angels, spirits, and guardians, your own insights and inspiration—to work with you and bring you . . . everything. Including information. Inspiration. I didn't know that joy and gratitude are somehow involved, as well as humble surrender to something bigger than yourself.

In love—the only way of Being.

ANONYMOUS

Years later, Anne became a friend of mine, and together with the mediums, she taught me how to give a reading. Anne is also the pastor of a Spiritualist church in another nearby Virginia suburb, Falls Church (and here it doesn't seem out of line to note that Washington, D.C., a political power center, is apparently a spiritual power base as well, boasting no fewer than seven Spiritualist churches that I know of, in addition to the thousands of other temples, mosques, synagogues, and churches of every denomination).

The Nine Spiritualist Principles

The National Spiritualist Association of Churches was formed in 1893 and promulgated the first six principles in 1899. They have revised them four times, the last in 1998:

1. We believe in Infinite Intelligence.
2. We believe that the phenomena of Nature, both physical and spiritual, are the expression of Infinite Intelligence.
3. We affirm that a correct understanding of such expression and living in accordance therewith constitute true religion.
4. We affirm that the existence and personal identity of the individual continue after the change called death.
5. We affirm that communication with the so-called dead is a fact, scientifically proven by the phenomena of Spiritualism.
6. We believe that the highest morality is contained in the Golden Rule: "Do unto others as you would have them do unto you."
7. We affirm the moral responsibility of individuals, and that we make our own happiness or unhappiness as we obey or disobey nature's physical and spiritual laws.
8. We affirm that the doorway to forgiveness is never closed against any soul here or hereafter.
9. We affirm that the precepts of Prophecy and Healing are Divine attributes proven through mediumship.

IT WAS A THIRD psychic and medium who introduced me to the history of spiritualism. So innocent was I that I'd never heard of the word, much less of the movement that had grown up in the late 1800s, in the wake of the intense interest in spirits and parapsychology that flourished in that century.

I'm not sure why the spirit world pronounced itself so prominently in the nineteenth century. Until then only Joan of Arc and maybe Emanuel Swedenborg admitted to hearing voices, communing with spirits. Even Saint Teresa of Ávila was circumspect. It may have had to do with witch-hunting and the Inquisition, but suddenly, in the 1830s, along came a royal flush of apparitions and spirits. In the United States, it started with a murder in the little hamlet of Hydesville, New York, and the lowly spirit that lusted for vengeance.

When the Fox family moved to their new farm on December 11, 1847, they had two children living with them: Margaret, fourteen, and Kate, eleven. The older children had already moved away. The following year the rapping started. Bumps in the night. Rapping had been heard in Germany once in 1520 and again in England in 1716, but the Fox family knew nothing about those, and finally on March 31, 1848, young Kate challenged the unseen entity (surely a demon!) to repeat the snaps of her fingers. "Here, old Splitfoot, do as I do." And it did. This caused a sensation! Every snap was echoed by a rap, until someone thought to make up an alphabetical code—one rap for A, two for B, and so forth—with which the entity laboriously spelled out the story of how he'd been a peddler who'd been murdered in the farmhouse and buried in the basement. That summer a party of men began to dig where the spirit had said his body was buried. They came across charcoal, lime, human hair, and the bones of a human skeleton, but it was not for another fifty-six years that the full skeleton was found in the old "spook house," together with a peddler's tin box, which you can see in the library at the Spiritualist community of Lily Dale in New York State.

After that a lot of people began to hear rapping and knocking.

The Fox sisters toured internationally giving readings to people, exhausting them with spelling out the alphabet. When the sisters were asked in one session why the spirits were communicating now, the answer came, "It is to draw mankind together in harmony and to convince skeptics of the immortality of the soul." (Alas! If history serves as a guide, it did no such thing; never has such slaughter been seen as in the following twentieth century.)

The Fox sisters got in way over their heads. One had a problem with alcohol, lost her child to her sister, who sued for custody; they were both attacked as frauds and for artificially creating the luminous substances seen in their séances, not to mention the table tilting, writing on slates, spirit lights, raps, and the appearance of disembodied hands. In one session recorded by Sir William Crookes, the distinguished investigator, Kate Fox's two hands were held by Sir William while her feet rested on his, and then—"a luminous hand came down from the upper part of the room . . . took a pencil from my hand, rapidly wrote on a sheet of paper, threw the pencil down, and then rose over our heads, gradually fading into darkness."

The Fox sisters died in the 1890s. By then the Society for Psychical Research had been founded by Sir Arthur Conan Doyle and other scientific giants of the time (1882), as well as the American Society for Psychical Research (1885), located in New York City, both of which engaged in scholarly research. In 1884 the College of Psychic Studies for experiential research was founded in London. And anyone can visit these august organizations even today or have a reading from one of the many psychics and seers who study and practice at the college.

Meanwhile other remarkable mediums and intuitives were cropping up, and charges of fraud continued, sometimes with cause. Sir Arthur Conan Doyle expressed it succinctly in his book *The History of Spiritualism (Complete)*: "there is no more connexion between physical mediumship and morality than there is between a refined ear for music and morality."

TWO OTHER INTUITIVE GIANTS must be mentioned, though they did not always speak to spirits. Daniel Dunglas Home, born in 1833 in a village near Edinburgh, was a contemporary of the Fox sisters. He moved to the United States as a child and returned to Europe as an adult. Artistic, refined, of delicate health, with a personal repulsion for anything sordid and ugly, he moved in the highest aristocratic circles of France, Russia, Italy, and England. He had extraordinary powers, possessing all four qualities that Saint Paul termed "of the spirit." We speak of a direct voice medium, a trance speaker, a clairvoyant, and a physical medium, this last having the ability to produce physical manifestations, and Home could do all four.

In one test, a small handbell was placed on the carpet, and it rang when nothing could have touched it; a glass of water held by the investigator above Home's head emptied mysteriously and just as strangely refilled itself, wetting the hands of the person holding it. Many times Home was seen to levitate and float, limbs rigid and his body in a nearly horizontal position, up to the ceiling (once marking it with a pencil) or in one case *out the sitting room window*, passing seventy feet above the street and then back inside. He went out headfirst and returned feet first.

Home was a deeply religious man. He gave readings to such clients as the authors Edward Bulwer-Lytton and T. A. Trollope (brother of Anthony Trollope), the socialist Robert Owen, and lists of dukes, counts, and other royalty, as well as ladies of the aristocracy. He took no money for his skills and died in poverty.

Home was investigated by Sir William Crookes (1832–1919), one of the leading chemical and physical scientists of his age, who began his investigations as a skeptic, believing everything was a trick, and against his best judgment was forced to confirm Home's abilities. (This is the same Crookes who investigated the Fox sisters as well.) Crookes reports that he saw Home levitate *at least fifty times*. Home could visit an art gallery, stand with his back to the wall, and describe the paintings behind him in detail. At his death the British press generally denounced Home as a fraud.

One last spiritual giant requires recognition, the controversial mystic and clairvoyant Edgar Cayce, known as the Sleeping Prophet. Born 1877 on a farm in Kentucky, he began at the age of six or seven to have visions, and in those early years he also had an invisible playmate who later went away. As a boy Cayce could fall asleep lying on his schoolbooks and on waking have a photographic memory of the contents. As he grew, so did his abilities. At the age of thirteen, he had a vision of a beautiful woman who asked him what he most wanted in life. He told her that, more than anything, he wanted to help others, especially children when they were sick.

He was a loving husband, the father of two children, a skilled photographer, a devoted Sunday-school teacher, and an eager gardener. Yet for forty-three years as an adult, Cayce would lie down, fold his hands over his stomach, and go into a meditative or "sleeping" or trance state, in which he could commune with people around the world and answer questions of every type, from hiccups to the secrets of the universe. He didn't know what he said in these readings. Gradually their range expanded from medical diagnoses to theology, education, soul journeys, spirituality, and psychology. After some years, with the help of a secretary, he began to keep records. To provide confidentiality, each reading was given a numerical code, and copies of 14,000 of his readings, guided by his wife and recorded by his secretary, are available to the public at the Association for Research and Enlightenment, Inc. (A.R.E.), a research body that he founded in 1931 in Virginia Beach, Virginia. In addition to A.R.E., he founded a hospital and a university.

As his fame increased, so did the demand for readings.

When individuals asked Edgar Cayce how to become more psychic, he answered that the goal is simply to become more spiritual, "for psychic is of the soul," he said, and as you become more spiritual, the abilities develop naturally. If the individual is not interested in spiritual betterment, he should leave the skills alone.

BY 1944, at the height of World War II, Cayce was giving eight readings a day, though even his own intuition urged him to offer no more than two a day, to slow down, stop. But sacks of mail streamed in each day, importuning him, and he felt such an obligation to ease the suffering he saw that he finally collapsed with a stroke. He died January 3, 1945, followed three months later by the wife who had supported and aided his work since their engagement in 1897, when Cayce was twenty and Gertrude in her teens.

He read the Bible once for each of his sixty-eight years, taught at Sunday school, recruited missionaries, and is said to have agonized over the issue of whether his psychic abilities—and the teachings that resulted—were spiritually legitimate.

Through his visions and readings, Edgar Cayce came to believe in reincarnation, and he found it compatible with the devotion he brought to Christianity. (There is compelling evidence for it. I refer you to the work of Dr. Ian Stevenson, psychiatrist at the University of Virginia, who has found three thousand substantiated cases of reincarnation worldwide.)

But what happens at death remains a mystery.

I'M AMUSED, BEMUSED, at people getting together to go out spirit hunting with their digital cameras and audio equipment, nightly stalking the haunted homes, churches, granges, and community centers reputed to house ghosts. They record the whispers of disembodied entities on tape or catch on film the orbs of light that will scientifically verify the invisible spirit presence.

"Hiiii," the hollow whispers come. (You hear it on the tape, clear as the breath they no longer have.) Sometimes they give a name.

"Who are you?" asks the amateur researcher.

"I'm Grace [or Doug, or Bill, or Naanceeey]."

Perhaps the tape reveals the squeak of a footstep, as if someone were treading on a loose board. Sometimes the camera shows streaks of light or orbs. Most images on the film are the products of dust, bugs, mist, fog, a camera strap, or misplaced thumb, but sometimes, I'm told, a discarnate spirit appears in the form of a blob of light. The ghost hunters are serious about their work and join clubs and leagues. The Mid-Atlantic Paranormal Research Council (MAPRC) is one such group, and its members are normal, ordinary folk. They are educated, informed, engaged, and curious—the kind of people you'd meet at any social function.

I have no interest in joining them. I find myself rebelling

against their work. What I'm saying is that I believe, and in the next breath don't, reverting to the protection of intellectual distaste. When I see a spirit myself or whenever I have a premonition or intuition myself, I believe. I trust. When caught up in the magnificence of a mystical encounter, I believe. But when something happens to the person standing next to me while I see nothing . . . I don't know what to think.

> *It is very difficult to rearrange one's ideas so as to fit these new facts in. Once one has accepted them, it does not seem a very big step to believe in ghosts and bogies. The idea that our bodies move simply according to the known laws of physics . . . would be one of the first to go.*
>
> ALAN TURING, mathematician who helped break the German Enigma cryptograph machine during World War II

SPIRITS, GHOSTS, DEVAS, POOKAS, and poltergeists—the superstition of it all! On one level I find these things revolting. Soon we'll be back in pagan times, when every tree and stump and spring and rocky cliff was thought to harbor its own god, to whom a traveler had better make appropriate sacrifice if he wished to pass unscathed.

And yet I heard my mother's voice after she'd died, calling me out of sleep by my childhood nickname: "Wake up! Wake up!" Urging me to hurry to meet my friends. And not long ago I stayed in the two-hundred-year-old house of a friend in Bucks County, Pennsylvania, where I was awakened in the night by a patter of fairy footsteps and then a sinking of the bed as someone sat down on it. *The cat,* I thought, even as I knew it was a spirit leaning over curiously to examine me. I was not afraid. It got up a moment later and drifted silently away: no cat.

It's a truism that before any scientific discovery is made its creative thinker is often despised, condemned. We think of Dr. Ignaz Philipp Semmelweis (1818–1865), then working in the Vienna General Hospital, who proposed in 1847 that the high death rate of mothers who delivered in hospital might be reduced if the doctors who moved directly from performing an autopsy to delivering the baby merely *washed their hands* in a chlorine solution before touching the mother. He found that this simple procedure reduced the deaths in his hospital from 10 percent to 1 or 2 percent. Nonetheless he was so vilified, humiliated, and harassed that he was forced to move to Pest. He ended his life in a mental institution, where in a twist of fate he died of the septicemia he tried to prevent. This was in 1864, before Pasteur discovered the germ theory that corroborated his insight.

Another example is William Harvey, who in 1628 declared that the heart acted as a pump, circulating blood throughout the body and that it could be heard as a pulse or heartbeat. His idea was considered ridiculous, since everyone knew that the body was controlled by humors, a theory propounded by the Greek anatomist Galen a thousand years before; and such is the power of suggestion that when the doctors of Harvey's time tried to test his outlandish proposal they really *could not hear the heartbeat* that would have proved his case.

fifteen

ENTERING THE FORBIDDEN

A man or woman who is a medium or wizard shall be put to death; they shall be stoned with stones, their blood shall be upon them.

LEVITICUS 20:27

FROM EARLIEST TIMES COME tales of gods and heroes who descended into Death's dark realm and returned to tell of it. According to the myths of ancient Sumer, a civilization that flourished from 5000 to 3000 BC in what is now southern Iraq, it took three days and three nights to travel to the Underworld and back. The goddess Inanna once did it, shedding a piece of clothing at each of the seven gates to Kur, until she arrived naked at the final portal, and alone. It is a fitting metaphor, for everyone dies naked and alone. In this long story, the goddess returned to earth for six months of every year but only because her sister volunteered to take her place for those six months.

Thousands of years later in the myths of ancient Greece, Persephone, daughter of Demeter, goddess of fertility, did not "go gentle into that dark night" but, captured by Hades, the God of the Underworld, was ravished and carried forcibly into the land of shadows. There, grieving and sorrowing, she refused to eat, while one tempting dish after another was placed before her.

Finally, to appease dark Hades, she sucked six small pomegranate seeds on her tongue and by that act was trapped, an echo of Inanna, for six months of every year, one for each seed. For six happy summer months each year, she returned to walk with her lovely mother, Demeter, and at each footstep flowers and plants sprang up behind them on the fertile ground, only to die again as Persephone departed for the next six barren months.

The god Adonis (do you hear the resonance of his name in the Semitic Adonai, "My Lord" or "Master," which is from an Ugaritic word meaning "father" or "lord"?) also descended into Hades, but he returned successfully, as did the semimortal Orpheus, who played the lyre so brilliantly that no living creature could withstand the charm of his music. Grieving for his beloved wife, Eurydice, Orpheus played for Hades, beseeching him to return Eurydice to life. So moved was the god of death that he granted the wish. All Orpheus had to do was walk back up the steep slope toward life, playing his music. Eurydice would follow, but whatever he did, Orpheus must trust and not look back. He walked that long difficult mile, playing and struggling against his doubt—Was she really behind him? Was he the brunt of a joke?—and made it almost to the throat of the passageway of death, when, unable to bear the tension any longer, he glanced behind, only to see the shade of his beloved, who, silently following, had acquired the heftiness of a substantial fog—as she faded, and slipped back into death.

Other heroes who challenged the dimension of death include Hercules (who had to capture Cerberus, the hound of Hades, in one of his near-impossible labors), Pythagoras, Theseus, and Pirithous. Odysseus, the crafty warrior of Troy, descended to the Underworld to consult Tiresias, the blind seer, and there he saw his own mother, who had died during his long absence at war. She scolded him as mothers do.

A thousand years later, in Virgil's *Aeneid*, the Trojan founder
of Rome likewise descended to hell, for by then no literary hero
could pass it by.

Glendower: I can call spirits from the vasty deep
Hotspur: Why, so can I, or so can any man;
But will they come when you do call for them?

HENRY IV, PART I, ACT III, 1:53–55

ALL THE ANCIENT CULTURES from Mesopotamia to the Celts
believed in divination, magic, and ways to win the favors of the
gods. Or to infer their will.

Magic refers to human efforts to affect nature and the gods,
and *divination* to gaining information about the future. In the
polytheistic world of ancient times, such practices were widespread (think of the famous oracle at Delphi in Greece). Only
the ancient Israelites prohibited divination, for God alone had
total control, communicating through his priests. To Israel divination was seen as an act of insolent *hubris* (if I may use the
Greek-root word) on the part of a human, of arrogance, the mark
of someone ready to elevate himself to the level of Almighty God.
The punishment was death.

But even in ancient Israel, the longing for supernal knowledge sneaked in. Speaking to spirits. Probing for the Will of God.
When the prophet Samuel died (note the slippery distinction
between divination and prophecy), and Saul became the new
(and first) king, almost his initial act was to banish all the wizards and seers, intuitives, psychics, and mediums from the land.
Soon after, the Philistine army gathered on the borders under

the leadership of A'chish, and David (of whom it was sung that Saul had killed his thousand but David his ten thousand), now Saul's mortal enemy, had raised his own army fighting on the Philistine side. When Saul saw the forces gathered on the plain, his heart failed him. He felt abandoned by God. He had neither dreams nor intuitions about what to do.

Then he sent a servant to go find the witch of Endor, a famous medium, who channeled a guiding spirit, or familiar, as it was called. Saul, disguised and hidden under the darkness of night, went to visit her with two companions. He asked her to call up her guide and have it bring forth the spirit of someone he would name.

The woman was no fool. *"Unh-unh,"* she said. "What is this, a trick to get me killed?" Saul swore by the Lord God Almighty (apparently forgetting the Third Commandment) that she would not be harmed. He promised. Then the woman went into an altered trance state.

"Whom shall I bring up from the Dead for you?" she asked. He answered, "Samuel." And when she saw Samuel, she gave a great cry and recognized her visitor as Saul. Saul asked what Samuel looked like, and she answered that he was an old man, covered with a mantle. Saul himself could see the spirit now, and he bowed to the ground at its feet.

"Why have you disturbed me?" Samuel demanded in raw irritation; and when Saul told him that the Philistines were making war, that he was afraid and that God had abandoned him, that he didn't have intuitions anymore, not even prophetic dreams, and that he needed help and what was he to do, Samuel lost all patience.

"Why do you come to me," he demanded, "seeing that God has departed from you and taken your kingdom and is giving it to David? You didn't listen to God, and this is what you get.

Tomorrow," he prophesied, "you and your sons and the whole Israelite army will be vanquished by the Philistines." Then he disappeared, and Saul fell flat on the earth, weeping and sore afraid.

Saul hadn't eaten in days. The kind woman of Endor prevailed on him to nibble some bread and partake of a calf that she killed and cooked for him to restore his strength.

The next day the two armies met. This was the battle in which all three of Saul's sons were killed (one being Jonathan, David's closest friend) and in which Saul himself was wounded by arrows. Saul asked his armor bearer to finish him off, and when the boy refused, Saul fell on his own sword and committed suicide, lest he be captured by the enemy and tortured and his corpse defiled. The armor bearer killed himself with Shakespearean inevitability, and the Israelite army was destroyed as foreseen by the so-called witch of Endor, the medium.

FROM AS FAR BACK as the fifth century BC, the Romans, likewise, opposed magic and witchcraft, which typically meant casting curses and spreading disease, or making crops fail, or concocting poisons and using them. But if they admired anything, it was divination, a practice their priests performed regularly, reading the entrails of butchered animals or watching for signs from the gods, such as a flock of birds flying past a pillar, or a rainbow at the right moment, or a comet passing over or a lunar or solar eclipse, all of which impacted human lives. Meanwhile the prohibition against magic and witchcraft continued, and fear of them ran high.

After the fall of Rome, in 476, the Frankish king Clovis promulgated the Salic law, which fined anyone tying a witch's knot or practicing witchcraft. So the prohibition goes back long before the later persecutions of the Christian Church. In fact, in its early years, the Catholic Church tried to stamp out the deep-rooted folk horror of witchcraft as rank superstition that encouraged violence, vigilante death squads, and atrocities. But gradually the Church began to equate witchcraft with heresy, the latter being important to destroy. Claims of secret meetings, orgies, feeding on babies, of flying through the air, or turning milk sour, of pacts with the Devil, rumors of desecrating the Eucharist, of shape-shifting and creating magic ointments were all considered signals of witchcraft and the occult. Horses found sweating in their stalls in the morning were said to be hag-ridden. By then no one knew the difference between sweet intuition and a paranormal experience; it all fell under the aegis of the forbidden. Joan of Arc was burned at the stake as a witch for hearing voices.

Beginning around 1450, the fear and prohibition became a mania that lasted for the next two hundred years. Millions of women were tortured and murdered during this fearful time: anyone with knowledge of healing herbs; anyone who admitted to having had a prescient or unusual dream or a crisis intuition; anyone who glimpsed an angel's wing, felt the upsweeping ravishment and joy of a spiritual experience—all were suspected of intercourse with the Devil. They were burned alive, drowned, hanged, or stoned to death. They were crushed with millstones on their chest. They were torn limb from limb, and if we are to believe the fairy tales, they may have also been hammered into nail-studded barrels and rolled downhill. If they survived the "test," lived through the drowning, for example, it only proved their witchiness, and they were killed a little more efficiently next time around. Any woman without a husband or father or brother or fortune to protect her was suspect, as was any woman who reached a certain age, for hags and crones were ugly, and ugliness a proof of evil. And this continued well into the 1700s. No wonder we still hesitate to talk of intuitions to this day, or psychic and paranormal experiences, much less of spirit entities.

> *"Oh, the devil, the devil," we say when we might be saying, "God! God!". . . I am quite sure I'm more afraid of people who are themselves terrified of the devil than I am of the Devil himself.*
>
> SAINT TERESA OF ÁVILA

Even today the prohibition against divination is rooted in our conditioning (*fortune-telling?!*), and you don't have to be Jewish to feel a nudge of something "wrong" as you sign up for classes, as if there are some things we're not supposed to know.

The few classes I've taken, though, were all and always about increasing your spiritual discernment, about widening your conscious contact with God, and growing spiritually. By which I mean growing in compassion and empathy, kindness and charity. The emphasis is on prayer, humility, and service to those in need. True, the teachers may suggest that you put a red light in your closet, the better to see a ghostly apparition; or they encourage the use of tools such as a pendulum or tarot cards, a Ouija board, a dowsing wand or crystal ball, or other forms of scrying. They may advise on what digital camera to use to capture the wispy image of an emanation. But these are merely aids for your own intuition.

At its highest level, the teachings are in no way a fortune-telling trick. It is purification and discipline that they urge.

Part IV

READING THE AIR

It is not I but the Father within that does these things.

JESUS CHRIST

sixteen

PERCEIVING

*Almighty God, unto whom all hearts be
open, all desires known, and from
whom no secrets are hid; cleanse the
thoughts of our hearts by the inspiration
of thy Holy Spirit, that we may perfectly
love thee, and worthily magnify thy holy
Name: through Christ our Lord. Amen.*

EPISCOPAL COLLECT

ONE NEW YORK PSYCHIC or intuitive who asked not to be
named gave a reading to the sister of a dear friend. The sister
wanted to rent an office for her business, and she had found a
site that seemed to fit her needs. He advised her to wait. Don't
take it. In a few weeks, he said, another opportunity would present itself that would be much better, and that's the one she
should rent.

Sure enough, in a few weeks the restaurant in the same building closed, and the space, which was larger than the original
office and with floor-to-ceiling windows overlooking the street,
came up for rent.

Some psychics have their gifts from earliest childhood, like
one I know, whose parents belonged to a Spiritualist church in
Baltimore and practiced giving readings on each other at home.
It was no more of a surprise that their son should demonstrate

psychic ability as a little boy than that Mozart, son of a musician, would have musical talent. Others have the skill from childhood despite the fact that no one in the family demonstrates the talent and may even be discouraged from using theirs. Others discover their gifts late in life after some remarkable experience, a mountaintop mystical experience, or (and this is true of many mediums) a loss or tragedy. Brenda Marshall, an English psychic who served for ten years as president of London's College of Psychic Studies, was one of these, acquiring her abilities only after the death of her husband, when, upon agreeing to work temporarily as a secretary at the college to help out a friend, she discovered to her amazement that she herself was psychic. Often it was her husband whom she felt guiding and supporting her during a reading.

And some people take classes and study with the industry of the young wizards at Hogwarts, developing their skill by hard work, the way a child learns to walk by falling down again and again and pulling himself up each time until he finds his balance and walks. No sense of failure for a child. A child learns to read the same way, studying the alphabet and putting the letters into words, until one day he can read deep philosophical treatises without even wondering how he does it. Everything takes practice, after all.

Still others discover their abilities by accident, as I did. I tell the story not to blow my own horn, for there are hundreds of thousands of psychics and mediums, and many with finer sensitivities than mine, but rather to illustrate the generosity of the Divine: God's grace lies everywhere. And once again we're reminded to turn all things over to God, asking only to serve unselfishly. Once again we're reminded to trust our intuition, those fragile whispers to the heart that come to us unbidden—gifts poured upon our heads, anointing us with oil.

It began some years ago. I had been in one of my troughs, between books with nothing to write (always difficult for a writer). As the months passed, I despaired that I wasn't *doing* anything with my life. I wanted to be of service. I wanted to be *useful* in some way. I prayed and prayed, asking for direction. Where was I supposed to be? What was I supposed to do? "Show me, show me." I prayed fruitlessly. And then, one morning I woke up from a sound sleep with the startlingly clear knowledge: "New York City. Six months."

And the leap of my heart, the purity of the *yes!* That I have come to associate with the Will of God.

My joy was followed instantly by doubt.

"New York City! I can't afford New York!" And then, the inward reproof and reminder: "Don't be silly. All things are possible with God."

That morning I phoned two people I knew in New York. One of them was a schoolmate I hadn't talked to in years. What made me think of her?

"I'm considering coming to New York for four or five months," I said, already bargaining down the time frame. "If you know anyone who has a furnished apartment to sublet . . ."

My classmate said, "I don't know of anything, but maybe Charlotte can help you. Here's her number."

It turned out that Charlotte was a real estate agent. I left a message on her answering machine at work.

That morning Charlotte was getting the mail in her building when a woman came up to her and said, "You do real estate, don't you? My friend Mary just died, and the family wants to find someone to rent her two-bedroom, furnished, rent-controlled apartment for six months."

When she got to work, there was my message on her answering machine. Coincidence? Serendipity? I only know that's how a stunning, two-bedroom rent-controlled apartment on the fashionable East Side came to me.

I went to New York with no idea why I was there or what I would do. Was I supposed to move there permanently? (No.) Was I to meet someone? I still don't know. But one of the people I met during this time was Charlotte, and we became close friends, living in the same apartment building. She was very sick. The doctors didn't know what was wrong. We talked a lot about death during the next months, though neither of us knew that within the year she would be dead, and I wonder sometimes if meeting her and the deep conversations we had late into the New York nights might be one reason why I was "sent" to New York.

Coincidence is God's way of performing a miracle anonymously.

ANONYMOUS

By coincidence, however, I'd been contacted just before moving to New York by the now-defunct organization Healing Works, which provided alternative healing to the poor and disenfranchised, to those who could not afford acupuncture, massage, psychotherapy, Reiki, cranial-sacral, or other healing energy modalities. It was run by Julie Winter, an exceptional woman who was a visionary, healer, intuitive, and therapist. And here is another example of the mysterious workings of God. How many little tucks in time and small coincidences were involved in orchestrating the convergence of our disparate lives? I offered to volunteer with them.

"What can you do?" Julie asked me, when I arrived to offer my services.

"Whatever you need. Lick envelopes, work the computers, help with your mailing lists—whatever would be useful to you."

She looked at me. She knew my books. "No," she said firmly. "I won't waste you on that. You'll give readings."

"Readings?" I was appalled.

"You can do it," she said confidently. "You have angels with you. I'll send you clients."

And that's how I spent the next four months, learning to trust my intuition and the words that fell from my mouth. To this day, I don't know why Julie knew I could do it. Was it intuition on her part, or did she simply understand that creative people have this sensitivity?

I DON'T THINK OF myself as a medium. I think of myself as giving an intuitive or spiritual reading. Sometimes (but not always) an angel appears and sometimes (but not always) a spirit. But sometimes I feel I am merely dipping into the client's history in some mysterious fashion that I don't understand myself.

Before she arrives, I ask the client to write down all her questions. It's not for me. I don't want to see the list. Rather, I want to make sure that she doesn't go away and later remember an important question: "Darn! I forgot to ask about such and such."

Before she arrives, I go into a prayerful state. I turn the coming session over to the Holy Spirit, praying that I may "hear" what is needed and speak words that will strike her heart, her soul. I pray for illumination. I pray for clarity, for a way to be of help.

I have one special place in my apartment reserved for meditation and for readings. When the client arrives, I settle her on the sofa, and I pray again, this time with her.

Straining or striving to "receive" an intuition or psychic illumination is useless. It throws up a brick wall and wards off the experience.

I ask to hold something imbued with the client's energy. It could be her ring or necklace, keys or watch. This practice is called *psychometry*, whereby you "feel" the history of an object. Every object carries an energy memory, as it were. Ambrose Worrall, the sensitive and healer, tells how once as a youth he picked up a curious metal bracelet and was struck by pain across his back, like the lash of a whip. The bracelet had been worn by a slave girl from North Africa who had been whipped to death. I know of one palm reader who holds the person's hand, but what she is doing is reading not the lines so much as the client's energy field, in the same way that I use a set of keys or a ring. Of course, some seers do not need to hold an object, and indeed I've given readings holding nothing. But psychometry is a method I feel comfortable with. Perhaps you've had the experience yourself. You are drawn to a particular jewel, or, conversely, you avoid wearing another one and can't for the life of you say why. If the client has brought no object, I hold the list of questions, folded into a tiny ball.

Now that we are settled, I write down the client's full name and date of birth. I take a breath and go into a slightly altered state, not a full trance. Am I using the delta brain waves? Theta? I have no idea. Words spill from my mouth. How do I know the things I say? It's beyond comprehension. But one thing I've learned to do is to speak exactly what I'm seeing, even if the vision makes no sense, for either it makes sense to the client, or else (and I myself have had this experience) she goes away and a few days later smacks her brow in sudden recognition: "Of course! *That's* what that was about!"

This is why I like the client to tape or write down everything that's said, for these are not my words, the language of my own limited understanding. They come from somewhere else, sometimes in a style that is often precise and different, using unusual words or imagery.

Often I don't remember afterward much of what was said. I cannot repeat the session, therefore, once I'm out of the altered state. I can only remember the gist of things and sometimes not even that.

Usually the first impression comes to me as a visual image, and I've learned to trust these swift metaphors, too.

I remember one of the first readings I gave in New York. I was still uncertain at the time that I could really do it. I settled the pretty young mother on a chair opposite me, took up the ring she offered, wrote down her name and birth date—and suddenly I saw a mouse scurrying around on the floor, here, there, everywhere, frantic, frenzied, changing direction every two feet. I could feel my heart pounding! It so startled me that I didn't know what to do. Did it have anything to do with this woman? I was by no means sure, but remembering to trust, remembering that I'd been taught to tell everything that came to me, I started to describe it, and the girl lifted her head, eyes filled with tears: "Yes, that's me. I can't stop running."

"We humans are porous." Mary Jo Peebles is a Washington psychotherapist who discovered this in her own work. "We pick up what is going on in others."

And still it doesn't explain the appearance of spirits.

I'M ASKED if I've ever received *nothing* in a reading. It's happened twice. The first time I was just beginning. The client was a woman in her early thirties, with strong black hair. I held her

ring in my closed fist. I closed my eyes and got . . . zero. Total
darkness. No sound. No taste. No sight. Nothing. Pitch-black.

Suicide is not an option. The words popped into my head, but
I wasn't about to say them out loud to her.

Finally I gave her ring back and admitted that I couldn't give
a reading. I didn't know why, but I wasn't "getting" anything. If
such a thing happened to me now, I'd speak bravely what I saw
and heard, but being so new I didn't trust my intuition yet. I
didn't know what to do. I offered her a healing Reiki treatment
instead, and she agreed. In this form of healing touch, the client
lies fully clothed on a massage table, while the practitioner
places her hands gently above or on her body. Energy flows into
the client. It is warm and soothing. It is golden in color or white.
It has an electrical energy, and it fills you, moving naturally to
those places that need healing. The practitioner doesn't need to
know or "do" anything. Instinctively her hands will tell her where
to move, send energy. Two or three times during the Reiki session the same words came to my mind: *Suicide is not an option.*

I'd never experienced anything like this before. I could tell
she was angry, depressed. Even the Reiki felt unsuccessful, for
the woman was resistant, deliberately and purposefully blocking
energy.

As she left, I held the door for her and unexpectedly blurted
it out: "Suicide is not an option."

She turned with the ferocity of a tiger! "How dare you!" she
cried. "What do you know? Who do you think you are?"

She left in a fury. She didn't deny the idea, and I felt miser-
able. I should have spoken up earlier, when we would have had
a chance to talk.

To this day, I don't know what happened to her. I phoned
Julia, who had sent her to me, and reported my concern. I was
told that her brother had committed suicide earlier and that her

therapist would be notified. I never saw her again, but I have not forgotten that single time when I met nothing but a dark void.

The second occasion came years later. A woman arrived for a reading, jaunty and electric with energy. She hooked her shoulder-length brown hair behind her ears and happily handed me her keys. I went into my slightly altered state, and for the second time felt . . . *nothing*. It was queer. Finally, in defeat, I returned the keys to her. I couldn't lie.

"I'm sorry. I guess I can't give you a reading. I'm not getting anything."

"Good!" She broke into a huge smile. "Now I know you're for real. They aren't my keys. That was a test. They aren't anything. If you'd given me a reading using those, I wouldn't have believed you. Here are mine. I'm ready."

Beforehand, I always feel I'm not going to "get" anything and sometimes I feel that way during the reading: no angels, no spirits, and not even much information. Often that's when people later write to tell me what a good reading they received. So what do I know? The whole process teaches humility.

SOME PEOPLE WONDER how the psychic gives bad news, and others may even refuse to visit an intuitive for fear of hearing information she hasn't strength to bear. But look. How do we know what is "good" or "bad"? Often the very things we claim to be "bad" come trailing clouds of glory, while those successes we trumpet as our triumphs may pierce our flesh with thorns. (My children have taken to asking their little ones, "What was the rose in your day, and what the thorn?"—a question that avoids all judgments of good and bad.)

In every life we face challenges. A crisis can be an opportunity. I speak of how best to rise to the occasion. I speak of wisdom, attitude, choices, and of strengths and opportunities, for these empower and offer hope.

How to Tell Someone He or She Has a Disease

I don't. I'm not a doctor. I might say, "Your health looks good," or "Have you seen a doctor recently?" But I will never offer a diagnosis or prescribe a remedy. I remember once seeing a kind of darkness at one client's belly. I suggested that she see a doctor, and when she did the doctor found polyps on her ovaries. But I avoid telling clients anything about their health, not only because of my own ignorance but also because of legal liabilities. It's not my place. It wouldn't be ethical.

EVERY CULTURE HAS a myth or legend or story about spirits. When Christ ascended, his spirit continued (continues) on this plane. Before, he was present to his disciples in the physical world and afterward as the Holy Spirit. The Dalai Lama notes that while Buddhist beliefs vary from culture to culture, Tibetan Buddhism affirms the special relationship between the emanation and its perception by another, and although "the emanation form of a human being may have ceased" he is still present in the form known as his *sambhogakaya*." He "continues to emanate and manifest in various forms that are most suited and beneficial to other sentient beings."

I HAVE HAD MEDIUMS tell me in a reading that a spirit has appeared. I find it hard to believe, unless they offer some means of identification. Anyone can say they see a spirit: "Oh, there's the most beautiful spirit here, a grandmotherly type. She has pink cheeks and the prettiest smile. Does the name Rose mean anything to you?"

"No."

"It doesn't matter. And there's a man here, too, a fine-looking gentleman. He has a wonderful smile. I think he's your father."

"Maybe." But one part of myself is cringing at descriptions that could hold true for anyone. Every man is a fine-looking gentleman or might be thought to be so. Moreover, the fact that the spirits usually don't have much to say does little to assuage my mistrust. But some mediums are truly gifted at naming spirits.

One of these, the late Gladys Strohm, was ninety-two when a friend gave me a reading with her. I had never heard of Gladys, but she was a large, extravagant, happy woman. (Why not? Like many spiritual people, she was joking with the spiritual dimension all the time!)

Gladys gave me one sharp, piercing glance as we walked toward her front door. "December twelfth," she blurted out, and then a year.

I broke out laughing. She'd just announced my birthday. "You do your research."

"No. It just comes to me."

We sat down, and with no preliminary prayers, no jotting down of names or dates, no psychometric holding of an object, not even a moment of quiet prayer and reflection, she rocked back in her chintz-padded chair and proceeded to tell me the first and last names of my mother and then of my father, and to describe them with frightening accuracy.

"They're both here. They just want to say they're watching, and they're very proud of you. They're together on the Other Side. Everything's fine. They're happy."

She then gave me a reading that I have referred to every now and again over the years, since so much of what she predicted has come to pass.

The Reverend F. Reed Brown, former pastor of the Arlington Metaphysical Chapel in Virginia, now retired and living in Roanoke, Virginia, at the campus that he founded, is also good at getting the names of attendant spirits and describing them punctiliously. In one reading, he heard the first names of both my parents and caught a close approximation of the unusual surname. For one friend of mine, a grandfather came through, complete with his Norwegian name—the same grandfather, I might add, who had sexually abused her when she was a little girl. He was not someone she cared to hear from, until she heard of the heartache and remorse he felt for his actions, now that he had passed over and learned more about the pain he'd inflicted, the evil he had perpetrated. It was after this conversation with him that she was able to let go, to forgive. Move on.

As for me, I'm not so good at receiving names. I have to ask for identification, some indication of the spirit's former life, something that makes sense if not to me then at least to the client who has come for the reading. And usually the entity complies.

One woman suddenly displayed a large green banner running diagonally from her right shoulder and across her chest to tie on the right hip. The word *Irish* thrust itself into my mind. All I could think was *Irish*. But it was enough for this daughter to recognize her first-generation Irish mother, who had belonged to Irish orders and marched in her green banner on St. Patrick's Day.

On another occasion a spirit appeared, claiming to be the client's husband. But how could we be sure? I asked her to think of something that would verify her husband's identity.

"The song that was playing when we met," she challenged.

"'Some Enchanted Evening,'" I answered without hesitation.

After which the spirit told his wife how to handle a financial problem puzzling her.

I repeat: A spirit does not always appear, for they are not our slaves, but I remember two events in particular. In one, I was giving a reading to a young woman, Sandy, when a girl appeared at my left elbow, asking to be heard. It was her sister. I was talking at the time about Sandy's relationship with her boyfriend. "Wait till I'm finished," I spoke to the spirit telepathically, and she stood patiently at my elbow, waiting.

I was still fairly new at giving readings. What if Sandy didn't have a sister?

"*Um.* Do you have a sister?" I asked cautiously.

"I did. She died."

"Well, she's here now." I was relieved. "And she wants to talk to you. But I think you don't need me. I think maybe you can feel her yourself."

"I *can!*" she cried. "I feel her."

"I tell you what. I think you won't need me to interpret. Talk to her. She can hear you. Tell her everything you need to say. I'll act as an antenna, holding the space for her, for you. If you can't hear her, tell me, and I'll pass on what she says, but maybe you can even hear her without me."

I felt myself reaching for a higher vibration, trembling, my whole body quivering. I was surrounded by light.

It turned out that Sandy could feel her sister's presence and talk to her, but she could not hear the answers. Then I received an astonishing bit of news: *You want me to say that?* The spirit was almost dancing foot to foot in her excitement.

"*Um.* She wants you to know she has a boyfriend on the Other Side."

Sandy was in tears. Her smile spread. "Oh, that's wonderful. She always wanted a boyfriend."

"Well, she has one now."

I don't remember much more about the session. After a while the spirit began to fade.

"Finish quickly," I said. "I can't hold the space much longer. She's leaving." And then she was gone, and my body stopped shivering. I returned to myself, already missing the pleasure of that heightened state, which was both difficult and exquisitely sweet.

Is this what the other mediums feel when they report, "There's a spirit here. She's a grandmotherly type, pink cheeks, so sweet . . ."?

I said that I particularly remember two spirit apparitions. The second one concerned a lovely woman in her late forties or early fifties, a stranger, who telephoned out of the blue. I will call her Suzanne. She asked if she could bring her husband. I answered no, that his energy would confuse her reading, but if he wished to come, he could sit in the next room while she and I had our session.

I don't know how I knew that; it was simply another example of perceiving intuitively a truth unknown before.

As it happened Suzanne's husband came with her, and I settled him in the other room while Suzanne and I went to my meditation alcove. I wrote down her name and date of birth, reached for her keys—and was so hit by a headache I thought I would faint. I felt nauseous. Could I even give the reading? This was the racking headache of Zeus, out of which sprang the goddess Athena. A moment later it occurred to me that the headache might not be mine.

"Do you have a headache?" I asked.

"No."

"Well, I have one, and it's like nothing I've ever known. It's so painful I'm going to faint." The next moment the spirit appeared. "Oh, there's a spirit here, a young woman. She's your daughter."

"I don't have a daughter," Suzanne replied stiffly.

By now the headache was gone. "Well, she's looking at you. She's saying, 'Mother. Mother.' You may not have a daughter, but to her you're her mother."

"I have a stepdaughter."

"I don't know. She's calling you 'Mother.'"

During all this time I felt myself uplifted, in that heightened state of energy I described earlier, in which my body is shot with electricity: I am clear; I am numb; I am both present to the client and yet not fully aware, straddling two worlds, one foot in each.

"She has a child with her." I described the baby, about a year old, tottering at her knee, clinging to her.

"What is she wearing?" said Suzanne suspiciously.

"Something brown, a kind of brown pantsuit. And boots."

"Can I bring my husband in?" she asked, and now her voice was fevered. "I think this is his daughter."

I agreed. The spirit told me to.

He sat in a nearby chair, and I watched, describing the spirit as she climbed into his lap and curled her arms around his neck, kissing and hugging him, clinging to him. He hardly needed my description, for he could feel her presence in his arms.

"It's how she always sat on my lap," he said. All three of us were weeping. It turned out that the young woman had been in the army. A year earlier, she had been walking from one building to another when she was struck by lightning and killed. She'd been pregnant.

This spirit stayed a long time, before it was time for her to go. Afterward, I gave a simple intuitive reading to the man and his wife but without any further dramatic apparitions.

"Oh, you're going to write a book," I remember saying, and not long ago I received in the mail a copy of the book she had written, together with a note saying that she and her husband were sailing on the long cruises that I'd also foretold.

I DON'T WANT YOU to think that having extreme intuition is any help to normal living. I heard of one psychic who came home after work one evening and sat down in the living room. It took him a few minutes to realize that none of the furniture looked familiar, that he was in the house next door. Embarrassed, he left, closing the door gently behind him, and walked across the lawn to his own house.

There's a reason Tiresias, the blind seer of ancient Greece, was sightless. Being psychic or intuitive doesn't mean that you necessarily are able to smoothly navigate your life. One brilliant psychic did not "see" that her second husband was sexually abusing her little daughter, and neither, after she had finally divorced him, was it easier for her to pick up the pieces. We all face life situations, ours to confront, and intuition comes in its own time.

THE ARRIVAL of an apparition is a powerful experience, but often the information received when giving a reading comes simply as a quiet, inner intuition. It makes me wonder: Is what I'm doing any different from reading body language and microexpressions, a host of subtle physical clues and energy fields? In some cases, I think not. After all, anyone who comes for a reading is troubled to a certain extent, confused. He's looking for a path. So, already you know a lot right there. Meanwhile, you are reading the tiny signals we all send out: a nod of yes, a confirmation, or the flash of a frown, a hesitation, or rejection of something said. Do you adjust? Of course you do. And yet it doesn't mean the insights are not right. Sometimes I find it easier to give a reading with my eyes closed or looking into some hazy middle space and not directly at the client's face.

For the first twenty or thirty minutes of a session, I ask the client to say *nothing* or not to speak until I pause and ask for information. For I find the client is often dying to spill everything, like jewels from a sack, to pour them into your lap. Some people, if they had their way, would take up the whole hour with their catalogue of problems and solutions.

I have three reasons for not letting the sitter speak immediately. First, my reading would be tainted by her revelations. Second, by listening, I would be thrown out of the slightly altered state wherein I attend to the whispers of intuition and can be of help. Third, having already told me everything she knows (or thinks she does), the client wouldn't trust the reading. How could she? Hasn't she already told me everything?

Sometimes I think I'm doing nothing special. A thought pops into my mind. Or doesn't. Sometimes I worry: *I'm not "getting" anything!* The information comes hesitantly, full of stops and starts. I have come to understand that *how* the information comes (via spirits, intuition, or psychic insight) is not important. My task is merely to pass on what I hear.

And sometimes the information comes through clearly. With certainty.

Years ago a woman named Jane came for a reading.

"Oh, your daughter's going to college in the fall! She's going to the University of Michigan!"

"She'd like to," Jane said, "but we can't afford it. She's applied to two other colleges now."

"No, she's supposed to go there. You have to get in the car

this weekend and drive to Michigan with her and talk to the financial aid office. This weekend. She'll get a scholarship."

"Can I telephone?"

"No. You have to go in person."

Fortunately Jane followed the advice of her spirit guides and drove to Michigan with her daughter, who received a hefty scholarship.

Recently Jane reminded me of another situation. She was working at an embassy here in Washington at the time and wanted to find another job. Clear as a bell, the information came: "Don't look. Let the job come to you. Something is coming along, but they'll call you." And in that same reading: "Don't forget to fight for your retirement."

"What?"

"Don't forget to ask for your retirement. You may have to fight for it."

"I don't think I get retirement. Do you mean in the new job?"

"I don't know. That's all I know."

"What retirement?"

"It doesn't matter. When the time comes, though, fight for it."

Later, as she left the embassy for her new position on Capitol Hill, she remembered that counsel, fought doggedly, and received the retirement pay the embassy had first refused to pay.

Where do the thoughts come from? What guidance puts these ideas in one's head? Not long ago I got a letter from a woman reminding me of a reading she had had a year before. At the time she had wanted to leave her job, because of two offensive supervisors.

"Stay," she was told. "It's a perfect fit for you. They're both going to leave. They won't be there long."

She wrote me to say that both supervisors had taken other

jobs and that everything had turned out as predicted. Now she loved her job.

Inviting Intuition V: Compassionate Observation

Here is another practice. Whenever you meet someone new, try for a quick "reading." It takes only the time to shake his hand—or glance up as he comes through the door. What do you know about the person? Guess. What is his profession? What is she worried about? Is he happy, excited, angry, frightened, or sad? What else can you "see"?

Don't worry about not checking your information. This is an exercise in developing empathy, in learning to listen. Later, you will be given the opportunity to check out your intuitions. The Universe will provide you chances, but only when you're ready and when no harm can come of it. Meanwhile, consciously practice an attitude of gratitude. Develop sympathy for others, empathy, compassion. I cannot stress this enough. I know plenty of people, many of them young, who are actually frightened of entering any unknown group. (What will they think of me? Do I look all right? They'll be talking behind my back!) If you start practicing this exercise in compassionate observation, you'll soon discover you have nothing to fear; they are probably not thinking about *you* anyway!

This also entails observing your own thoughts. Are you gossiping? Why? Is it to feel superior or righteous, or is it out of true concern for your own friend? The more you are aware of your own feelings and the more tender you become, the more readily do psychic powers appear.

The Gift of Mistakes

In your early days of listening for whispers, you may mistrust the messages, or else you let reason override a warning that's as weak as the shimmering of a leaf. Perhaps your intuition makes no sense. You bull past it, ignoring the signals, inattentive to such psychic signs, and thus *by your mistakes you learn the signals*, and that's another gift right there.

Some people beat themselves up for making a mistake, but I say no, give thanks for them. By your mistakes, you learn in what form your intuition comes to you.

WHAT DOES ALL THIS MEAN? Is there Fate? Predestination? Destiny? I believe we make our future, choice by choice, each moment of the day. I believe we're given a general map, a soul map, if you will, but we have absolute Free Will to follow or decline the plan. What's important is to listen to the nudges of your inner wisdom, leading you to higher consciousness. I believe that our task is always to become more "spiritually mature." And what does that mean? To be less angry, less prideful, less greedy, less intolerant, less violent. To have more patience, serenity, compassion, inner tranquillity, simplicity, and happiness.

> *It is very hard to be simple enough to be good.*
>
> RALPH WALDO EMERSON

I MUST CONFESS THAT in the beginning I doubted these visions, visitations, insights—everything. I reported them to the client, yes. But I would finish a reading, see the individual out, and then in despair run over and over it in my mind, whatever I remembered of the reading, doubting everything. Today, I've learned to trust my guidance and not look back. I am a conduit, that's all, and what the client does with the information is also not my responsibility. For you have Free Will *not* to accept or act on what the intuitive sees. I know several people who paid for readings with renowned psychics and ignored their every word.

I never doubt the guidance I receive at the time of a reading. It's important to be detached from it. I see myself simply as a vessel through which the information flows. That also releases me from carrying the memories and concerns about it. This is perhaps one of the most difficult things for many mediums to learn. I was fortunate to have a teacher who insisted on this discipline. I encourage any medium to develop it too, because it's not healthy to carry concerns after the reading.

ANNE GEHMAN, medium

Ethics

The *ethics* of psychic readings are basically the same as those of normal living: Do unto others as you would have them do unto you.

Be truthful. Be kind.

Do not give a reading if you are emotionally shocked, angry, or in distress.

Don't give a reading without permission. Don't go marching up to someone at a dinner party or a business convention

and declare that you've just received some psychic information he needs to hear: Believe me, he doesn't!

And never ever "look into" someone without permission.
(Note that this injunction is different from practicing your intuitive skills in an effort to discern microexpressions and body
language. If you wish to develop psychic skills, do so by sending and receiving telepathically with a friend, or gather four
or five people together expressly to practice your perceptive
and projective skills. It's wrong to impose on strangers.)

Finally, as an intuitive, you never kiss and tell. I heard of
one psychic who, needing money, decided to write a tell-all
book in which she'd spill the secrets of the famous congress-
men and celebrities who'd come to her for readings, naming
them all. Fortunately, the project came to nothing, for it was
totally unethical!

ALL THESE STORIES RECOUNT my successes and none of my
failures. Is that because I don't remember the times I've failed?
Or are the clients too kind to throw my misses in my face? One
thing you learn in giving readings is to be gentle with yourself,
especially while you are learning. Forgive yourself. You may need
to practice forgiving yourself daily (another spiritual discipline).
Giving readings is an imprecise skill. You see through the glass
darkly, snatching moments of illumination before the mists roll
in and boundaries close.

But one thing is certain. You love the client during a reading.
You merge in surprising ways, and if she or he is receptive, the
two of you can travel to the stars.

seventeen

RECEIVING

*To know ourselves truly, to acknowledge
our uniqueness, we need to be known
and acknowledged by others for who we
are. We cannot find the way to true
freedom and life in secrecy. We need
loving and caring friends with whom we
can speak from the depth of our heart.*

HENRI NOUWEN

MEANWHILE THE PROSPECTIVE CLIENT, too, has responsibilities.

F. Reed Brown tells how a man once came to him for a reading, already disdainful, skeptical, and searching for the signs of fraud. Who knows why he came for the reading in the first place, given his distaste? Perhaps his wife sent him. Perhaps he was intent on uncovering a fraud. He was a Civil War historian, and during the reading, the spirits of one Civil War soldier after another appeared, Union and Confederate, offering their names and how and where they died, while the client grimaced, sneered, and tossed his head.

"What a waste," Brown commented. "Here he was, an historian, given the crown jewels of research. All he had to do was go look up the Civil War records to find out if the names and material were for real. Instead he grabbed his tape and left in a huff."

"Does it affect you? When someone's suspicious?" I asked.

"Of course it does. I can't give as good a reading if I have to fight off the client's disdain. It's about energy. It's energetic."

Later the man stormed back into the office of Dr. Brown, waving the session tape.

"How did you do that?" he demanded, furious.

"Do what?"

"How did you get that voice on the tape?"

"What voice?"

He played the tape of the session, on which Brown could be heard talking, when suddenly a different voice interrupted: "Listen to him, Sidney. He's trying to tell you something!"

"How did you do that?" he shouted. Defiant, suspicious, angry at not receiving the explanation of fraud that he demanded, he asked to examine the office while Brown went to lunch.

When Dr. Brown returned from lunch he found his office trashed: drawers pulled out, papers strewn over the floor, the pictures torn from the walls, everything helter-skelter. The skeptic found none of the wires or devices he expected.

WHEN YOU COME for a reading, it's incumbent on you to be respectful. Out of courtesy, you should be on time and follow whatever directions you are given by the psychic, intuitive, or medium. You should attend to the reading with dignity. I'm not telling you to set aside your gifts of critical judgment. If the reading doesn't ring true or feel "right," if the psychic sends bad vibes, if your intuition starts clanging warning bells and waving lanterns up and down the tracks to stop the oncoming train wreck, then get up, even in the middle of the reading, and *leave!* Trust your gut. Pay and depart. You're under no obligation to stay.

Especially is this true if you feel the psychic is trying to pull you into additional sessions, to con or frighten you, whether by insisting you return for healing treatments or more readings or for him to cast out demons that he sees in you. Not everyone has moral integrity.

But when the seeker finds a good psychic (and there are many thousands), someone who has been recommended by a friend or by word of mouth, and when in making an appointment you test your intuition, your inner guidance, to ensure the psychic or medium "feels" right, then treat the practitioner with respect.

Remember that skepticism affects a reading. Just as physicists find the researcher's attitude influences experiments with subatomic particles, so do your thoughts and ferocious negativity affect the clairvoyant. So please don't heave great sighs or frown or jiggle or snort in disbelief. If that's the way you feel, don't come for a reading!

A second courtesy: The client should leave when the session is over. This is sometimes hard to do. For that full hour you have been "seen" and understood in ways most people rarely experience, and as part of the process you may feel love and approval. The psychic cannot give a reading without conjoining with the client at some deep unconscious level. It's flattering, seductive. You don't want to leave. You think up other questions merely to extend the session, to remain in this sacred space a moment more. But unless you are paying for the psychic's time, it's not quite fair.

Moreover, the intuitive may likewise be unable to break free easily. Certainly it's hard to charge for additional time, though this can extend an extra fifteen or twenty or thirty minutes. He has your check in hand; how can he look at his watch and say, "That'll be another X dollars, please"? In a way, separating after giving a reading is similar to that period after making love when you and your partner float in the embers of each other's embrace, feeling your energy fields drift and sift, as you slowly pull apart, each into your own physical body. If your partner jumps up brusquely, it feels like tearing a piece of paper in two. In giving a reading you've merged at a subconscious level, and afterward you need to come back into your own separate zones, inside your boundaries. Thinking about money at this stage is hard.

I exaggerate perhaps to make my point. But the client's responsibility at the end of the session is simply to pay and leave. I know one medium who has had such trouble with people departing that now she charges for every five minutes over the initial hour. She's tough, but she's learned the hard way how her time and energy can be eaten away by a client wanting more.

Only connect.

E. M. FORSTER

I'VE ALSO KNOWN PEOPLE who have asked for readings at inappropriate times. "Oh my gosh! You're a psychic! Can you give me a reading right now? Here at this dinner party?" They don't mean to be disrespectful. They speak out of ignorance or playfulness, without understanding the deep subconscious levels into which the psychic sinks when giving a reading.

"I only have one question—this won't take a minute," she says, calculating also that it may not cost as much as a full reading either. (No point wasting a whole hour! Not when you only have one teensy question.)

It doesn't work that way. Most psychics are unable to answer the quickie "just one question" on target (right this minute) with anything better than ordinary commonsense advice—hardly what the client wants. The intuitive doesn't know what information will come to him, drawn from the deep subconscious levels, and usually a reading covers considerable ground. Some psychics won't even consider the quickie request: "I don't do that," they will say.

FINALLY WE COME to the question of how to find a good psychic or intuitive.

First, ask around. Do you know someone who has gone to this intuitive? What was her experience?

Second, use your own intuition. Hold the name of the psychic on your tongue. Taste it. Is it sweet? Is it tart or bitter? Or try one of the methods I use when vacillating between two choices. Go into a prayerful state. Hold out your hands, palm up. Imagine the two choices placed one in each hand. Which is heavier? Darker? Which hand sinks? Which has a lighter, light-struck feel? Which emits a sense of happiness and joy? Choose the lighter, joyful one! Do the same with the names of two psychics: Which one "feels" right? Pray over the decision, asking for the highest good for all concerned. I say this knowing, however, that periods of stress and lack of clarity are exactly those times when your intuition isn't working well. Which is why you want to consult an intuitive in the first place.

Very well, then, what should you look for?

First, look to see if the information given is specific and correct. Second, you judge her life, her surroundings, her words, and thoughts. Look for someone with the highest principles and spiritual aspirations whose purpose is to guide others on their spiritual way. Look for someone who is completely at peace, someone with high ethical and moral standards, wisdom, compassion, and a strong feeling for her clients' welfare. Look for someone who is happy, serene, fulfilled.

Be sensible. Charlatans and frauds abound. Take the case of Hong Kong's Nina Wang, one of Asia's richest women, who died in 2007, leaving her $4 billion fortune not to her family but to the ex-bartender and feng shui expert Tony Chan, who is accused of pretending he could magically extend her life with his secret rituals and supernatural powers. Especially guard against someone trying to get you to throw money at them.

In the end you rely on the salty gift of ordinary common sense.

CODA

WHAT DO WE MAKE, finally, of these musings on intuition and the paranormal? What meaning are we to gather? I think that what we learn in considering these flashes of intuition that fall on us like Byron's wolves (or the Assyrian cohorts in purple and gold), these psychic sighs and insights of the soul, these meta normal senses, is the unwavering reality of survival after death. It's nothing new. A vast body of experience from earliest times attests to it, whether it is the certainty of some afterworlds, the many mansions in Our Father's lands, or reincarnation back into these planes and plains. Poets, philosophers, scholars, scientists, great intellects—all concur in upholding truths as old as history itself. Plato, the Bible, Blake, Shakespeare, Wordsworth, Dante, the Christian mystics and Buddhist monks, the Sufi ecstatics and songs of Mirabai, the greatest minds the world has ever known, names of impeccable integrity— are all in agreement on the indestructibility of consciousness. Christ died physically, and yet He continues to emanate and manifest as Christ-consciousness in ways most beneficial to all. The Buddha died. His last words concerned the transient nature of all things, including even the body of a fully enlightened being, validating the doctrine of impermanence. Yet his presence continues as pure consciousness.

Intuitively or instinctively, we recognize that with all our differences, the vast diversity and variety of life, we form One spiritual whole: earth, animals, humans, cosmos—all pure Intellect, all derived from the mystery of Great Intelligence. How different we all are and yet how alike! Connected. We experience our lives under the illusion of separation, while underneath, as if half waking from a dream, we dimly hear the sirens singing of mystical Union and Unity, its strands interweaving into one glorious silver web, supporting us. Breathe on one fine strand, and ripples run across the whole: not a thread, no matter how thin or how far away, that does not shiver with the whisper of that wind, that sigh, that *psi*. Our minds reach out to one another even across vast distances and years, islands in the sea. We are not trapped inside our bodies like a lobster in its shell. There are no limits to our minds, our intuition, our transcendent knowledge.

Many of us sense the palpable presence of sources invisible, that of angels and guides and guardians and totems, of spirits and spiritual sages, all unseen. They speak through us. Gentle. Guiding. Or perhaps it's the inner beauty of our own hearts.

As the years have passed some of the distrust of psychics and the paranormal has eased. Formerly, almost any investigation into psychic matters, telepathy, psychokinesis, clairvoyance, clairaudience, premonitions and prescient dreams, physical manifestations of spirits, including knocking and rapping and writing on slates, flashing lights and wispy apparitions ridiculed, regarded with suspicion.

Today we find a different danger: an explosion of public interest, sometimes at a superficial level, that tempts us to forget that these intuitions are intended for our spiritual, not psychic, development. You will have many experiences as you proceed on the spiritual path, and in general these *siddhis* should be ignored.

Concentrate instead on what they point to: the psyche, the Soul, the Holy Spirit. Concentrate on the goodness that underlies the universe.

According to Zen stream of thought, humans were created because the gods needed a form that could witness and articulate the sheer wonder and beauty of life.

What is *spiritual?* Like *love,* the word's been diluted by overuse. I think it means first an appreciation that there is something greater than our petty selves. Call it by whatever name you like, a Higher Power or Creative Intelligence, a Spirit of the Universe underlying the totality of things. Call it by one of the thousand names that we ascribe to holiness, be it God or Allah or Krishna or the Buddha, His Majesty, Avalokiteshvara, Christ. It means, too, a recognition that we share in those same qualities, and as we work throughout our lives to cut away the detritus that hinders that recognition, we find ourselves with powers beyond imagining: intuition . . . and the understanding that it's simply that, a skill, like cooking a good meal, like fertilizing a tomato plant, like training a fine dog—just another expression of the miraculous luminous experience that lets us know that we're alive.

I wish we had a host of words for *love* and the subtlety of emotions it evokes, the poignancy, ecstasy, fragility, breath-held wonder, and humility that go with it. If intuition rides on ribbons of love, we need a word for this. I've heard that the Japanese have many words for *rain,* making translation from English difficult. We say, "The rain fell against the windowpane." What kind of rain? the Japanese translator asks. Is it a sad rain, a driving rain, a poignant rain, a lighthearted spring rain, an angry, lashing storm, a forlorn or grieving rain? So attuned is the Japanese language to the emotions that I understand there's a word to describe the feeling you have when standing on a beach gazing at the sun as it sets over the darkening sea. English, on the other hand, is full of martial nouns: *table, chair, lamps*. We need more words in English to express emotion and the spiritual, intuitive, nonmaterial dimension, luminous words that whisper to us of the soul, words quivering in the silence of their invisibility.

ACKNOWLEDGMENTS

Once an admirer asked the artist James Whistler as they stood before one of his paintings, "How long did it take you to paint that?"

"All my life," he answered.

That's what I feel like as I approach the end of writing this book and consider those who have helped, to whom I would offer thanks and public acknowledgment. The list stretches out endlessly, even eternally, if you add the immortals who have influenced me over the decades of my life. It's like the ever-widening, outward-spreading ripples of a rock tossed into a pond. Those closest are my family, beginning with my mother and father, my wonderful brother and sister, my beautiful daughters and their husbands, and then I add the outer-running ripples of in-laws and cousins, nieces, nephews, and of friends so close they may as well be sisters and brothers: too many to list. Do you know who you are? Add my writer-artist friends, who form a little brotherhood, sharing professional insights, dismay, anguish, helplessness, encouragement, calling to one another, sometimes across huge distances, with kindness and support.

Begin with these: I wish to thank my agent, Anne Edelstein, who first approached me with the seed of the idea that became this book, and to Krista.Ingebretson; to Sara Carder, my sensitive editor at Tarcher, and her assistant, Andrew Yackira, who was also of inestimable help. I thank Julia Cameron and Katherine Neville, Catherine Mayo, Peggy Heller, Suzy Kane, and Anne Simpkinsen, and my assistant, Jane Swensen, and especially Judith and Jo, Jackie Simpson in England, Jim and Lori Williams in Texas, Anne Gehman, Dean Radin, Christie Vinson, Barbara Culliton, F. Reed Brown, Larry Lonergan, and all the other people who put up with me during the incubation, gestation, and delivery of this book. To all those who are named in the book, who freely gave me their stories of intuition, spread petals in my path, passed me notes of where to look; and to all those unnamed, the richness of whose influence cannot even be imagined, I give you thanks. The reader will come across numerous people in this book. To all of you, I am grateful, my heart so full, I bow down at your beautiful feet.

Here: a rock tossed in the pond. *Thunk!* I hope the ripples lap against your chairs and lick you with the knowledge of how much you helped, how much your life has influenced another.

appendix i

HOW TO MEDITATE

Do you want to increase your intuition? First you must quiet the mind. Grow still. One way to do this is to practice meditation. Meditation brings three things:

First it brings peace and calm. Second it brings laser-sharp concentration and intuition. You know things. Third, if you wish it, it leads to the direct experience of God. There are many forms of meditation. Weeding the garden can be a form of meditation; knitting, running, rowing— any quiet, repetitive, mind-calming activity can be considered meditation.

Everything in our culture, however, is designed to keep you in a rushed and churning state of mind: cell phones, iPods, blogs, e-mails, children, the stress and pressure of work, faxes, phones, bills, banking, red tape . . . How hard it is to find a moment's peace! In the beginning you should practice meditating for only five or ten minutes at a time. That will be hard enough.

Sit comfortably in a chair. (You don't have to be cross-legged on the floor.) Your back is straight, your head parallel to the ceiling, your chin neither tucked tight nor lifted up in such a way that you put pressure on the back of your neck. You feel easy, floating on your sit bones.

Take a breath. Scan your body, and wherever you feel discomfort, breath out with awareness into that place.

Now put a smile on your face.

Focus your attention gently on your nostrils and watch your breath: in . . . out . . . you count. In . . . out . . . Instantly your mind will leap off to a thought, a doubt. It can't stand to be trapped, chained, restrained. Gently bring your attention back to your breath: in . . . out . . . Remember to smile. This is beautiful.

All you are doing is *witnessing* yourself, observing. You take two breaths. Your mind runs off, and it may take you a few moments to realize you're lost in planning or daydreaming or making lists or remembering something that happened yesterday. Don't be upset. *Planning*—you name the action of your mind, or it may be *dreaming, judging, remembering, analyzing.* Or perhaps it's an emotion that carried you away. Notice and name it: *fear, worry, anxiety, jealousy, anger, resentment, compassion, joy, happiness, criticizing, boredom, desire for a cup of tea.* Always, go back to your breath. If it is a physical sensation that captured your attention, you name that, too—*pain, pressure, prickling, tickling, itching, soreness*—and once more, without judgment or dismay, return your awareness to this present moment. For the breath is the only thing we know to be true, this moment, this one breath.

At the end of five or ten minutes, stop.

Give thanks, get up, and go about your day, refreshed.

Gradually, as your mind learns to slow down, become alert and aware, you will increase the period to twenty minutes once a day and then, if you wish, to two sessions, morning and evening, and you'll look forward to these periods of relief.

Don't worry. Be at peace. What you are doing is mind training, and, like training a puppy, it takes time. Within a week, you may build up enough strength to remain in meditation for ten or twelve minutes, but there's no hurry. Soon your jumpy, frantic mind will come to love this period of rest and will settle instantly into peace. At this point you may want to remain in meditation for longer periods—an hour, two. But you don't *need* to meditate for more than twenty minutes at a time. Soon—quickly—your intuition will sharpen. You know how to do things that previously baffled you. You solve problems during meditation: how to speak to your children, what question to ask the accountant, when and how to present an idea to your boss.

Meditation opens the gateway to your inner wisdom.

Be grateful.

Be easy.

Be at peace.

appendix ii

RESOURCES & RESEARCH

There are so many books, periodicals, classes, films, and other resources on creativity, intuition, the brain, and *psi* phenomena that I offer here only a bare skeleton of suggestions. Some are easy; some are pretty heavy going; some are personal favorites. But as you delve into the topic, you'll find hundreds more that you like, and better. This list is just a beginning. Don't forget the Internet

GENERAL

Andreasen, Nancy C. *The Creating Brain: the Neuroscience of Genius* (New York: Dana Press, 2005).

Baba, Meher. *Gift of Intuition*. Fifteen essays compiled by Don E. Stevens (London: Companion Books, 2006).

Brizendine, Louann, M.D. *The Female Brain* (New York: Morgan Road Books, 2006).

Cayce, Edgar. *My Life as a Seer: The Lost Memoirs* (New York: St. Martin's Press, 1997).

Davies, Paul. *The Mind of God: Science & the Search for Ultimate Meaning* (New York: Penguin, 1992).

Dossey, Larry, M.D. *The Power of Premonitions: How Knowing the Future Can Shape Our Lives* (New York: Dutton/Penguin, 2009).

Giesemann, Suzanne. *The Priest and the Medium* (Carlsbad, CA: Hay House, 2009).

Gladwell, Malcomb. *Blink: The Power of Thinking Without Thinking* (New York: Little, Brown/Hachette, 2006).

Goodall, Jane, with Phillip Berman. *Reason for Hope: A Spiritual Journey* (New York: Warner, 1999).

Hagerty, Barbara Bradley. *Fingerprints of God: The Search for the Science of Spirituality* (New York: Riverhead, 2009).

Jawer, Michael A., with Marc S. Micozzi M.D., Ph.D. *The Spiritual Anatomy of Emotion* (Rochester, VT: Park Street Press, 2009).

Kandel, Eric R. *In Search of Memory: The Emergence of a New Science of Mind* (New York: Norton, 2006).

Karagulla, Shafica, M.D. *Breakhrough to Creativity: Your Higher Sense Perception* (Camarillo, CA: DeVorss, 1967).

Main, John. *The Heart of Creation* (New York: Continuum, 1998).

Myers, Isabel Briggs, with Peter B. Myers. *Gifts Differing: Understanding Personality Type* (Mountain View, CA: Davies-Black Publishing, 1995).

Myers, Isabel. *Introduction to Type: A Description of the Theory and Application of the Myers-Briggs Type Indicator* (Gainesville, FL: Center for Applications of Psychological Type, 1990).

The Myers-Briggs Type Indicator. Online at: *www.myersbriggs.org/my-mbti-personality-type/mbti-basics/*.

Nimmer, Dean. *Art from Intuition: Overcoming Your Fears and Obstacles to Making Art* (New York: Watson-Guptill, 2008).

Quenk, Naomi L. *Essentials of Myers-Briggs Type Indicator Assessment (Essentials of Psychological Assessment)* (Gainesville, FL: Center for Applications of Psychological Type, 2009).

Radin, Dean. *The Conscious Universe: The Scientific Truth of Psychic Phenomena* (New York: HarperOne, 2009).

————. *Entangled Minds: Extrasensory Experiences in a Quantum Reality* (New York: Pocket Books, 2006).

Sheldrake, Rupert. *Dogs That Know When Their Owners Are Coming Home and Other Unexplained Powers of Animals* (New York: Crown, 1999).

————. *A New Science of Life: The Hypothesis of Formative Causation* (Los Angeles: Tarcher, 1981).

Wise, Anna. *The High-Performance Mind: Mastering Brainwaves for Insight, Healing, and Creativity* (New York: Tarcher/Penguin, 1997).

Worrall, Ambrose A., with Olga N. Worrall. *The Gift of Healing: A Personal Story of Spiritual Therapy* (New York: Harper & Row, 1976).

ENERGY AND AURAS

Eden, Donna, with David Feinstein. *Energy Medicine* (New York: Tarcher/Penguin, 1998).

Emoto, Masaru (*The Hidden Messages in Water*, trans. David A. Thayne) (Hillsboro, OR: Beyond Words Publishing, 2004).

Ledwith, Míceál, and Klaus Heinemann. *The Orb Project* (New York: Atria Books/Beyond Words Publishing, 2007).

Peirce, Penney. *Frequency: The Power of Personal Vibration* (New York: Atria Books, 2009).

CONTROLLED REMOTE VIEWING

Buchanan, Lyn. *The Seventh Sense: Secrets of Remote Viewing as Told by a "Psychic Spy" for the U.S. Military* (New York: Pocket Books, 2003).

Morehouse, David. *Psychic Warrior* (New York: St. Martin's Press, 1996).

Problems, Solutions, Innovations, www.crviewer.com.

Schnabel, Jim. *Remote Viewers: The Secret History of America's Psychic Spies* (New York: Dell, 1997).

SPIRITUALIST AND PSYCHIC RESOURCES

Barker, Elsa (written in 1914 through her hand). *Letters from the Afterlife: A Guide to the Other Side* (Hillsboro, OR: Beyond Words Publishing, 2004).

Barnes, Peggy. *The Fundamentals of Spiritualism* (Summit, NJ: Stow Memorial Foundation, 2002).

————. *Psychic Facts* (Summit, NJ: Stow Memorial Foundation, 2002).

Burroughs, H. Gordon. *Becoming a Spiritualist* (Lily Dale, NY: National Spiritualist Association of Churches, 1962).

Choquette, Sonia. *Diary of a Psychic: Shattering the Myths* (Carlsbad, CA: Hay Press, 2007).

————. *The Psychic Pathway: A Workbook for Reawakening the Voice of Your Soul* (New York: Three Rivers Press, 1994).

Doyle, Arthur Conan. *The History of Spiritualism (Complete)* (Middlesex, England: Echo, 2006).

Hoffman, Enid. *Develop Your Psychic Skills* (Alglen, PA: Whitford Press, 1981).

King, Margaret L. *Mediumship and Its Phases* (Lily Dale, NY: National Spiritualist Association of Churches, 2002).

Peirce, Penney. *The Intuitive Way: A Guide to Living from Inner Wisdom* (Hillsboro, OR: Beyond Words Publishing, 1997).

Riva, Pam, ed. *Light from Silver Birch* (London: Psychic Press, 1983).

Roberts, Jane. *The Afterdeath Journal of an American Philosopher: The World View of William James* (Englewood, NJ: Prentice-Hall, 1978).

Wallis, E. W., and M. H. *A Guide to Mediumship and Psychical Unfoldment* (Whitefish, MT: Kessinger Publishing, 2006).

White, Stewart Edward. *The Betty Book: Excursions into the World of Other-Consciousness Made by Betty Between 1919 and 1936* (Columbus, OH: Ariel Press, 1988).

— ——. *The Unobstructed Universe* (Columbus, OH: Ariel Press, 1988).

IN BRITAIN

I also recommend to anyone who can get them some of the periodicals from the College of Psychic Studies in England, especially their publication *Light: A Review of Spiritual and Psychic Knowledge*, which has been published without a break since 1881.

The College of Psychic Studies, 16 Queensberry Place, London SW7 2EB. Tel: 020 7589 3292.

www.collegeofpsychicstudies.co.uk/light

Look also for *Paranormal Review: A Forum for Debate*, the magazine of the Society for Psychical Research, 49 Marloes Road, Kensington, London W8 6LA. The Society conducts scholarly research into human experiences that challenge contemporary scientific models.

www.spr.ac.uk

The Arthur Findlay College at Stansted Hall, calling itself the foremost college for the advancement of Spiritualism, is a full board residential center where students develop psychic abilities and study Spiritualist philosophy and practice.

IN AUSTRALIA

The Chiara College of Metaphysics, established in 1995, has online classes as well as in five locations. Mailing address: PO Box 6145, Hammondville, NSW 12170, Australia. E-mail: admin@chiaracollege.com.

IN THE UNITED STATES

The American Society for Psychical Research (ASPR), 5 West 73rd Street, New York, NY 10003 (Tel. 212-799-5050). Established 1885, the ASPR is basically a research library.
This is balanced by the following:
The New York City Skeptical Psychic Society, founded February 2010, has occasional meetings at 20 West 20th Street, New York, NY, or on Facebook.
The Parapsychological Association of scholars and scientists studying *psi* phenomena, founded in 1957 by J. B. Rhine, publishes the *Journal of Parapsychology and Mindfield*. This association held its 53rd annual convention July 2010 in Paris.
The Association for Research and Enlightenment (ARE), 215 67th Street, Virginia Beach, VA (Tel. 800-333-4499). Founded by Edgar Cayce in 1931, this is one of the world's greatest resources for the study of transpersonal subjects, spirituality, dreams, intuition, *psi* abilities, philosophy, and reincarnation.

INTERNET

There are dozens of local spiritual schools and colleges in every
country in the world and thousands of psychics available
through the Internet or Facebook who are willing to teach
their skills. Being unfamiliar with them, I hesitate to make
specific recommendations. But I am sure that courses at any
church that is part of the National Spiritualist Association
would probably be legitimate.

If you look on the Internet, you will find some 3.15 million hits
under "Psychic Societies NYC" alone. I wish we had in the
United States an equivalent to the long-established English
colleges for the study of psychic abilities and mediumship.
But we do have numerous schools. Click on *www.Psychic-Junkie.com* to find listings of psychic and spiritual schools that
offer B.A., M.A., D.D., and Ph.D. degrees in metaphysics,
distance learning, and psychic development. Remember, you
are on your own. Use your intuition. Test the teaching. It is
spiritual development that should be of concern, not the acquisition and use of heady powers.

Good luck!

INDEX

If you enjoyed this book, visit

www.tarcherbooks.com

and sign up for Tarcher's e-newsletter to receive special offers, giveaway promotions and information on hot upcoming releases.

TARCHER
PENGUIN

Great Lives Begin with Great Ideas

New at **www.tarcherbooks.com**
and **www.penguin.com/tarchertalks**:

Tarcher Talks, an online video series featuring interviews with bestselling authors on everything from creativity and prosperity to 2012 and Freemasonry.

If you would like to place a bulk order
of this book, call 1-800-847-5515.